The Music of Creation

D1157501

The Music of Creation
with CD

Arthur Peacocke & Ann Pederson

Fortress Press
Minneapolis

THE MUSIC OF CREATION, with CD

The authors and publisher acknowledge with deep gratitude the assistance of the Templeton Foundation in funding selections for the accompanying CD.

Unless otherwise marked, scripture quotations are from the New Revised Standard Version Bible, copyright © 1989 by the Division of Christian Education of the National Council of the Churches of Christ in the USA and used by permission.

Scripture quotations marked (KJV) are from The New King James Version, copyright © 1979, 1980, 1982 Thomas Nelson, Inc. Used by permission. All rights reserved. Scripture quotations marked (NEB) are from The New English Bible, copyright © 1961, 1970 by the Delegates of the Oxford University Press and the Syndics of the Cambridge University Press. Reprinted with permission. Scripture quotations marked (REB) are from the Revised English Bible, copyright © 1989 by the Oxford and Cambridge University Presses, Used by permission.

"The Bright Field" originally published in: R. S. Thomas, *Laboratories of the Spirit*. London. MacMillan 1975. Used by permission.

Lines from "Dry Salvages," in *Collected Poems* 1909–1962 by T.S. Eliot, © 1963 by Harcourt, Inc., copyright © 1964, 1963 by T.S. Eliot, reprinted by permission of the publishers Harcourt Inc. and Faber and Faber Ltd.

Cover photos: Music © Brand X / SuperStock. Spiral Galaxy M51 ("Whirlpool Galaxy"), © R. Kennicutt (Steward Observatory, Univ. of Arizona)
Cover and interior design: Becky Lowe
Permissions and CD development: Lynette Johnson

Library of Congress Cataloging-in-Publication Data
Peacocke, A. R. (Arthur Robert)
The music of creation, with CD / by Arthur Peacocke and Ann Pederson.
    p. cm.—(Theology and the sciences)
ISBN 0-8006-3756-9 (alk. paper)
    1. Creation. 2. Religion and science. 3. Music—Religious aspects—Christianity. I. Pederson, Ann. II. Title. III. Series.
BS651.P333 2005
231.7'65—dc22

                                                                                    2005015203

The paper used in this publication meets the minimum requirements of American National Standard for Information Sciences—Permanence of Paper for Printed Library Materials, ANSI Z329.48-1984.

Manufactured in the U.S.A.

10 09 08 07 06   1 2 3 4 5 6 7 8 9 10

Contents

*To David Lumsden and Gary Pederson
to whom the authors have been, respectively,
immensely indebted over the years
for their sharing of their
musical wisdom and insight*

Prelude

Music is that which cannot be said but upon which it is impossible to be silent.
    Anonymous, attributed to Victor Hugo

The man that hath no music in himself,
Nor is not mov'd with concord of sweet sounds,
Is fit for treasons, stratagems, and spoils;
The motions of his spirit are dull as night,
And his affections dark as Erebus:
Let no such man be trusted. Mark the music.
    Shakespeare, *The Merchant of Venice*

Music is the sole domain in which man realizes the present. By the imperfection of his nature, man is doomed to submit to the passage of time—to its categories of past and future—without ever being able to give substance, and therefore stability, to the category of the present.
    Igor Stravinsky, *An Autobiography*

All art constantly aspires towards the condition of music, because, in its ideal, consummate moments, the end is not distinct from the means, the form from the matter, the subject from the expression; and to it, therefore, to the condition of its perfect moments, all the arts may be supposed constantly to tend and aspire.

Walter Pater, *The Renaissance*

Now, what is music? This question occupied me for hours before I fell asleep last night. Music is a strange thing. I would almost say it is a miracle. For it stands halfway between thought and phenomenon, between spirit and matter, a sort of nebulous mediator, like and unlike each of the things it mediates—spirit that requires manifestation in time, and matter that can do without space. . . . The essence of music is revelation; it does not admit of exact reckoning, and the true criticism of music remains an empirical art.

Heinrich Heine, *Letters on the French Stage*[1]

*T*hese quotations—and a host of others could have been culled from the anthologies— illustrate some of the varied appraisals of music. Somehow music is experienced as conveying insight, wisdom even, but in a way that is inherently ineffable, mysterious, and beyond the capacity of words, as such, to explicate. Music shares this paradox with the experience of the divine, called by whatever name. It is not surprising therefore that music and religion—the experience of the transcendent in the immanent, and of the immanence of the transcendent—have been intricately intertwined both culturally and in the lives of individuals. The expression of religious devotion through music in liturgy and ritual has been a marked feature of all human cultures. In the West, the development of music as a vehicle of both personal and communal experience has been especially sophisticated and subtle, with works of individual composers playing an influential role. This development has inevitably included many outstanding expressions of, in particular, Christian devotion and aspirations, and these continue to merit intensive study, analysis, and performance.

It is not this aspect, however, of the role of music that we wish to offer in this, our "composition." Rather, we have both found ourselves impelled, from within a common theological perspective but with different cultural backgrounds, to note the remarkable and fruitful parallels of key features of music and of music-making with especially contemporary aspects of Christian life and thought. Arthur Peacocke, as a scientist and theologian, has found that the forms of music and its relation to humanly experienced time afford a rich reservoir of models and metaphors for explicating God's continuous creative activity and presence.[2] Ann Pederson, a theologian and musician, has been struck by the way in which her experience of corporately creating music, jazz in particular, has features that reflect very closely, and thereby enrich, the way in which we can understand how creative Christian community should develop and operate.[3]

Music is a universal language, especially with today's electronic and radio communication. The experience of music can be communally uniting whether it be at a Promenade Concert in London, England, in the Festspielhaus at Bayreuth, Germany, or at a blues club in Chicago, Illinois. It is widely recognized, however, that, certainly in the West, the explicitly verbal language of the Christian understanding of creation, God, humanity, nature, and the Christian community falls increasingly on deaf ears so that the need for a rebirth of pertinent and potent images, models, and metaphors expressing Christian perceptions becomes increasingly urgent.

We not only share a love of music and similar understandings of Christian thought and life, but also find that music affords us a rich resource for reflection on those understandings as well as yielding ineffable experiences, popularly denoted today as "spiritual." The following is a joint "composition" in that we have linked Arthur Peacocke's thinking to the theme of creation and creating with and in time (the first and second movements and, in the more explicitly Christian-oriented bridge passage), to Ann Pederson's ideas about communal and ongoing creativity (the third movement and coda). We have listened to and critiqued the other's composition, not least in the choice of music associated with our texts, and urge readers not to postpone but to listen to the corresponding tracks on the CD as they read the text. We hope to shed light on God and creation through the rich creativity we see in music. We are especially thankful to the Templeton Foundation for making it possible for us to include this vital element in our work. To aid readers in making these connections, we have also included a glossary of basic musical terms.

The whole composition is an attempt to share our experiences with those who love music and who are seekers after the divine Presence—the Transcendent-in-the-Immanent and the Immanence-of-the-Transcendent—both in the passing world and in fleeting human experience.

First Movement

CREATION WITH TIME

Whosoever is harmonically composed, delights in harmony; which makes me much distrust the symmetry of those heads which declaim against all Church-Musick. For my self, not only from my obedience, but my particular Genius, I do embrace it: for even that vulgar and Tavern-Musick, which makes one man merry, another mad, strikes in me a deep fit of devotion, and a profound contemplation of the first Composer. There is something in it of Divinity more than the ear discovers: it is an Hieroglyphical and shadowed lesson of the whole World, and creatures of God; such a melody to the ear, as the whole World well understood, would afford the understanding. In brief, it is a sensible fit of that harmony, which intellectually sounds in the ears of God.

   Sir Thomas Browne, *Religio Medici*, 1642

*T*hree heavenly visitors move like a Greek chorus through Bertolt Brecht's play *The Good Person of Sichuan*. They are trying to find at least one apparently "good" person in the whole world and, when they think they have succeeded,

1

she turns out to have maintained her good deeds only by playing a double role to keep herself alive by doubtful means, in order to have the opportunity for doing good. The play ends with a dramatic cry from this failed-but-trying-to-be-good person: it was one word—*Help!* This cry of the human heart is evoked by intense personal, social, and natural tragedies of the kind most of us scarcely know where to begin to sort out. To do so we have to start a long way back to begin unraveling a little the entangled threads of our existence and to discern more clearly the warp and weft that underlie it.

Most of us can recall how, as we grow through childhood, we begin to acquire a sense of our self-identity and to ask "Who am I?" and, perhaps later, "What am I here for?" This growth in our sense of self is paralleled by a growing awareness of the world as distinct from this newly discovered self and we wonder at the sheer givenness of the world in which we are set. No one has expressed the child's sense of wonder at the glory of the existence of the world around us more eloquently than the seventeenth-century writer and priest Thomas Traherne:

> Is it not strange, that an infant should be heir of the whole World, and see those mysteries which the books of the learned never unfold? The corn was orient and immortal wheat, which never should be reaped, nor was ever sown. I thought it had stood from everlasting. The dust and the stones of the street were as precious as gold: the gates were at first the end of the world. The green trees when I first saw them through one of the gates transported and ravished me, their sweetness and unusual beauty made my heart to leap, and almost mad with ecstasy, they were such strange and wonderful things.[1]

Before and behind the desolation and tragedies we experience, there does indeed lie the sheer givenness and wonder of the world. We are all impelled to ask the mystery-of-existence question that haunted the Ionian Greeks when science was born: "Why is there anything at all?"

The profound prose poem of the first chapter of Genesis is a response to this perennial human question. In it, "God" acts directly by "letting be" the different kinds of existence. "And God said, Let there be . . . ; and there was . . ." (Gen 1:3 KJV) is how God is depicted as creating "the heavens and the earth" (Gen 1:1 KJV). In that seminal work, the relationships between the things that are thereby given existence are established simply by a commanding word of the Creator: "And God made the firmament and divided the waters. . . . *And God said,* Let the waters under the heavens be gathered together. . . . *And God said,* Let the earth bring forth . . ." (Gen 1:6, 9, 11 KJV). This manner of creating is echoed much later in the Bible in the prologue to the Gospel of John: "In the beginning was the Word, and the Word was with God, and the Word was God. The same was in the beginning with God. All things were made by him; and without him was not anything made that was made" (John 1:1, 2 KJV). Here the "Word" (*Logos,* in Greek) is God in God's mode as Creator; and scholarship has shown that in the author's milieu this *Logos* was a conflation of the active, creative, self-expression of the "word-of-the-Lord" of the Hebrew God, and the inbuilt principle of the rationality of the world that the Greeks saw as especially reflected in human rationality, which was thereby empowered to discern that basis of universal, cosmic order.

However, these traditional considerations, potentially richly significant as they indeed are, still leave most of us with a lacuna in our imaginative resources for explicating what meaning could, or might, be attributed to speaking of God, the Ultimate Reality, as "giving existence to" something other than Godself, that is, to everything that is. There is an enigma concerning this emergence of reality from the nonreal, this birth of the temporal from the nontemporal. Can a more "local habitation and a name" be given to this coming-into-existence that might be grasped more intuitively?

We suggest that the experience of music can afford the very imaginative and metaphorical resources we need to enrich our apprehension of creation. The mystery and wonder of the opening of Franz Joseph Haydn's *The Creation*, for example, splendidly tracks the Genesis text (CD track 1). Pertinently, "Ring out, ye crystal spheres," calls Milton in his *Ode on the Morning of Christ's Nativity*, thereby reminding us of the ancient notion that the rotation of the planets made a harmonious sound, humming the joy of God in creation. The idea goes back to Pythagoras, who identified the numerical relation between the harmonics of a string with that between the orbits of the planets. And the ancient Hebrews, too, thought of "the morning stars" singing together in a chorus of joy at creation: "Whereupon are the foundations [of the earth] fastened? or who laid the cornerstone thereof; When the morning stars sang together, and all the sons of God shouted for joy?" (Job 38:6, 7 KJV). Today we are much more likely to ask: "Why does the world manifest the implicit rationality and beauty that the scientist and artist discern?" or, perhaps, more directly influenced by science itself, "How did there come to be matter, energy, space, and time, all so closely related in Einstein's famous equation?"

We might well think it hopeful to turn to science for answers to such fundamental questions about our very existence. Science is, in fact, concerned with *origins*, that is, in tracing the existence of everything as far back *in* time as it can go. The sciences can indeed extrapolate back some 13 billion years to that singularity popularly called the Hot Big Bang when all matter and energy were concentrated in a minute space of unimaginably high density and temperature. From this point in our clock time the universe expanded forming the space our radio telescopes scan today.

But what happened at or before the Hot Big Bang? Theoretical physicists—recognizing the intimate interlocking of space, time, matter, and energy—strain to penetrate this question, the most difficult of all the questions that nature poses, by attempting to combine into one theory the well-established theories of fundamental physics: quantum mechanics, relativity, and gravitational theory. Although they have had some successes with postulating that there was an inflationary period of extremely rapid expansion that preceded the expansion astrophysicists have been able to track, this does not settle the basic problem about the emergence of matter-energy in space-time. Currently there is intense investigation and speculation about a "grand unified theory" (GUT) unifying the fundamental four natural forces and even of a "theory of everything" (TOE).[2] But would they explain why there is anything at all? Scarcely, for in principle they cannot say *why* the relationships and laws are actually what they are and *why* they should operate at all because answering those questions is not *logically* necessary. Beautiful and intellectually exhilarating though the GUT and TOE will be if and when discovered, they would still not explain their own existence and efficacy.

We are not asking what happened before the Hot Big Bang since our clock time itself is so inherently related to the emergence of matter-energy, but we are asking why there should be relationships of this kind at all that might begin to explain the origin of the universe with time. There can be no scientific account of the very existence of a universe of this kind because all-that-is is contingent, all could have been otherwise.

It is in response to such questions that we affirm that the world does not just happen to be—that it owes its origin to an ultimate Being. The "doctrine of creation," as it is more formally called, is *not* about what happened at a point *in* time and space since both of these are aspects of the created order. The affirmation that the world is created is a positive response to the question of why there is anything at all. To affirm that the world is a creation means that it is in all time and in every space given existence, and has been endowed with being and becoming by an ultimate self-existent Reality other than itself—that Reality we name, in English, "God," who transcends all that is created. Although the sciences cannot account for the actual existence of the world, their success, which is based on the application of human rationality and experiment, does confirm the underlying unity and oneness of all-that-is. They point to the world's being intricately interconnected in space and time by regular relationships often expressible in terms of mathematics. Moreover, the world is richly diverse in its manifestations, in both living and nonliving systems. So the source of its existence, "God," must be of unfathomable richness—a diversity in a profound unity. From current scientific perspectives it is also possible to infer other aspects of God in relation to what is created, but they cannot illuminate the enigmatic phrase that we have, perhaps too slickly, been using up till now, namely, the suggestion that there is One who "gives existence to" all-that-is—space, time, matter, and energy in their cornucopian forms.[3]

The panorama of the cosmos that the natural sciences have now unveiled for us is one of greater splendour, evocative of yet more awe, than anything that any human generation has ever before been privileged to experience, and it would have delighted our ancient forebears. It is the aim of this book to show how features of music and the experience of it can enrich, inform, and stimulate our imagination and intuition of the nature of divine creation of the world—a world now revealed to us by the sciences as affording an even richer and more profound context for the image of God as the supreme Creator-Composer, the incomparable Improviser, than we have ever had before.

CREATION AS A COMING INTO EXISTENCE

The notion of creation as a coming into existence at once raises the question of *in* what existence occurs and also what it is *that* comes into existence.

Patterns Coming into Existence with Time

We consider first how music, and the experience of it, might illuminate the notion—fundamental to many religious traditions—that the real is created out of the nonreal, that is: creation by God is *creatio ex nihilo*; all-that-is and all-that-has-been and, indeed, all-that-will-be is "given existence" by an Ultimate Reality that is other than what is created. The principal stress, for example, in the Judeo-Christian doctrine of creation is on the dependence on God of all entities and events: it is about a perennial relationship of all-that-is to God, and not about the beginning of the Earth or of the whole universe at a point in time. It is an affirmation that any particular event or entity would not happen or would not be at all were it not for the sustaining creative will and activity of God.

One can begin to grasp what this means by recalling an incident in that rich mine of philosophical wisdom: Lewis Carroll's *Through the Looking-Glass*. You may recall how Alice, behind the looking glass, encountered the two pugilistic boys Tweedledee and Tweedledum and how, in a contentious conversation with them

she checked herself in some alarm, at hearing something that sounded to her like the puffing of a large steam-engine in the wood near them, though she feared it was more likely to be a wild beast. "Are there any lions or tigers about here?" she asked timidly.

"It's only the Red King snoring," said Tweedledee.

"Come and look at him!" the brothers cried, and they each took one of Alice's hands, and led her up to where the King was sleeping. . . .

"He's dreaming now," said Tweedledee: "and what do you think he's dreaming about?"

Alice said "Nobody can guess that."

"Why, about *you*!" Tweedledee exclaimed, clapping his hands triumphantly. "And if he left off dreaming about you, where do you suppose you'd be?"

"Where I am now, of course," said Alice.

"Not you," Tweedledee retorted contemptuously. "You'd be nowhere. Why, you're only a sort of thing in his dream!"

"If that there King was to wake," added Tweedledum, "you'd go out—bang!— just like a candle!"

"I shouldn't!" Alice exclaimed indignantly. "Besides, if *I'm* only a sort of thing in his dream, what are *you*, I should like to know?"

"Ditto," said Tweedledum.

"Ditto, ditto!" cried Tweedledee."[4]

The Red King, like the author Lewis Carroll, was simply dreaming them into existence in something of the same kind of way Christian theology has long affirmed that God thinks all-that-is into existence with time. One of the most influential attempts to understand the relation of God, time, and creation was that made by Augustine in his *Confessions,* where he addresses himself to those who ask, "What was God doing before he made heaven and earth?" This provokes him to undertake a profound analysis of our experience of time. From it he concludes that the world was created along *with* and not *in* time. Time itself is a feature of the created cosmos and therefore no act of creation can be located at a point within created time itself. There is no time without events and God's eternity is not just endless temporal duration but a mode of existence that is qualitatively different from our temporal experience. Augustine addresses God thus:

How could those countless ages have elapsed when you, the Creator, in whom all ages have their origin, had not yet created them? What time could there have been that was not created by you? How could time elapse if it never was? You are the Maker of all time. . . . It is therefore true to say that when you had not made anything there was no time, because time itself was of your making. . . . Let them see, then, that there cannot possibly be time without creation.[5]

Since Einstein—and in accord with this ancient insight—time, along with space, matter, and energy has had to be conceived as inherent in and intrinsic to the very nature of the created world and closely interlocked, as the equations of relativistic physics that relate them continue to be corroborated. God, as the self-existent Ultimate Reality, is thus to be conceived as giving existence to each segment of time, "all the time," as it were. That is, if God ceased to will the existence of each successive moment with all its events and their interrelations, they simply would not *be* at all. So time is in itself a positive intrinsic feature, not an evil one as some have alleged, of a creation declared to be "very good" (Gen 1:31 KJV) in the Judeo-Christian tradition.

Many have been accustomed to think of "creation" as an event *in* time—at, say, 4004 BCE if we follow Archbishop Ussher in the eighteenth century, or even 13 billion years ago if, like many astrophysicists today, we confuse the Hot Big Bang "origin" with that creation. So the notion of creation *with* time does not come at all easily. It is at this point that music can be an imaginative resource as we find hinted at in an evocative passage from C. S. Lewis's Narnia novel *The Magician's Nephew*, where he describes how earth-dwellers and the Witch witness the coming into existence, the founding, of the new world of Narnia:

"Hush!" said the Cabby. They all listened. In the darkness something was happening at last. A voice had begun to sing. It was very far away and Digory found it hard to decide from what direction it was coming. Sometimes it seemed to come from all directions at once. Sometimes he almost thought it was coming out of the earth beneath them. Its lower notes were deep enough to be the voice of the earth herself. There were no words. There was hardly even a tune. But it was, beyond comparison, the most beautiful noise he had ever heard. It was so beautiful he could hardly bear it. . . . Then two wonders happened at the same moment. One was that the voice was suddenly joined by other voices; more voices than you could possibly count. They were in harmony with it, but far higher up the scale: cold, tingling, silvery voices. The second wonder was the blackness overhead, all at once, was blazing with stars. They didn't come out gently one by one, as they do on a summer evening. One moment there had been nothing but darkness; next moment a thousand, thousand points of light leaped out—single stars, constellations, brighter and bigger than any in our world. There were no clouds. The new stars and the new voices began at exactly the same time. If you had seen and heard it, as Digory did, you would have felt quite certain that it was the stars themselves which were singing, and that it was the First Voice, the deep one, which had made them appear and made them sing.[6]

Here Lewis evokes the image of music emerging as it were out of silence, from a nothingness that, like the silences in music, proves to be fecund in giving substance to the creation of successiveness—for sheer uniformity could never elicit a sense of time and time certainly involves successive entities and relationships. However tentative, elusive, and incomplete, there needs to be some sense of the coming into existence of *succession*, of instants of existence of those entities and relationships.

But *from* what may God be said to be creating? The "nothing," the *nihil* referred to in the classical assertion that God creates *ex nihilo*, is indeed nonexistence and can be depicted only by what it lacks—it is without time, timeless, and without order, a chaos where no forms have duration warranting their being described as existent, as entities capable of being named, the "'formless void" of the opening of Genesis

(1:1). It is such a nothingness, such a timeless state, that Haydn depicts musically, and remarkably, in "The Representation of Chaos," the slow orchestral introduction to his oratorio *The Creation* (CD track 1). With outstanding originality he used what might at first seem the recalcitrant, formal resources of late-eighteenth-century classical music to create an impression of formlessness and therefore ambiguity and a sense of mystery. Technically, it is a tour de force of shifting keys; of resolutions by cadence, deferred and never completed, frequently dissolved by suspensions and passing and grace notes; and of cheating our expectation of the return to a putative tonic by the use of many tonal centers. The alternation of pianissimos and rests with fortes and fortissimos echoes the enigma that is the essence of creation—the nothing giving rise to something. It is an explicit example of what philosopher of science Karl Popper has affirmed: "a great work of music (like a great scientific theory) is a cosmos imposed upon a chaos—in its tensions and harmonies inexhaustible even for its creator."[7]

Because Haydn was not just steeped in, but one of the originators, of the classical style of the 1790s, the work is not, on critical analysis, entirely formless. Indeed, just before the narrating angel, Raphael, starts the oratorio by announcing "In the beginning God created the heavens and the earth," it superbly evokes the sense of fragments of order appearing kaleidoscopically, hinting at a sense of succession and therefore the emergence of segments of time. Patches of ordered patterns in the form of short arpeggios are almost randomly dispersed throughout this "representation of chaos."

It is tantalizingly significant that it is also a rising arpeggio that dominates the supreme musical instantiation of the coming into existence, with time, of patterned order in the unique opening bars of the Prelude to *Das Rheingold,* the beginning of Richard Wagner's Ring Cycle (CD track 2). At first, the nothingness of the pregnant silence of the audience is usually, and certainly in Bayreuth's Festsprelhaus, almost palpable in its intensity of anticipation. Then, not so much from the abysmal depths of earth and sea as from before the dawn of time, comes an E-flat from eight double basses and then bassoons—so quiet and low that it is felt through the skin rather than heard through the ears—followed by an almost painfully long pause ("Is that it?" we begin to wonder). Then a succession of very low, faint notes in a rising E-flat major chord. Persistently, imperturbably, relentlessly the horn notes ascend, building up the chord—calm but swelling in volume and gathering momentum, with strings and woodwinds until they merge into a reiterated stream of undulating sound (arpeggios) to become the music of the surging, swirling waters of the Rhine River. Thus, the audience has been witnessing the beginning of the world, the emergence of the first state of nature—for that chord based on E-flat (in both its major and minor forms) is the basis of all the subsequent motifs in the Ring Cycle that represent the idea of nature in its various manifestations.

The curtain rises and we find ourselves submerged *in* the waters of the Rhine. Water is the symbol of the primordial chaos at the world's beginning in the ancient Babylonian and biblical myths. In those myths order is created from the mythical waste of waters; in the Ring Cycle primal form arrives with the native progeny of the Rhine, the Rhine maidens, whose voices float above its lower pulse. Wagner has conducted us, subtly but surely, from nothingness into primal form with time. Indeed, it has been said that this Prelude also echoes the later, collateral emergence of time, not only with form as such, but more pertinently with the unfolding drama of gods and humanity, with self-consciousness and all its potential hazards—as soon becomes apparent following the Prelude in the encounter in the first scene between the Rhine maidens and the lustful and thieving dwarf, Alberich.

Moving Patterns Coming into Existence with Time

These musical examples exemplify—and give precision and meaning to—another aspect of the mysterious creation of time: how the potential becomes manifest.

We perceive through them that time is sensed only through what is experienced as movement, the movement of shifting patterns—something that was the same *becomes* different. The existence of time is established with the emerging *movement* out of nothing; to be movement is to be movement of something, so that entities come into existence with process. In both musical examples so far, the arpeggios—at first fragmentary in Haydn's "The Representation of Chaos," then explicit in Wagner's "Prelude"—are gradually woven into and give way to larger units that are transformed into even richer complexes.

The ebb and flow between these new patterns of sound at their various stages of elaboration—a kind of polarity, differentiation, and articulation—is like the rhythm of breathing. In these pieces and in Creation itself there is first the undifferentiated, the inchoate, then a gradual transformation into identifiable and perceivable forms possessing duration, followed by patterns of periodic exchange in the succession of these forms, which begin to be articulated as distinct entities. These latter constitute the discrete organizing beats of rhythm, the birth of which characterizes created time with its content of created entities. Rhythm unfolds the possibilities of polarization and differentiation that time possesses and, just as breathing is essential to life, rhythm is essential to creation.

Thus it is significant that images of breath, spirit, and wind appear in the opening of the Genesis account of divine creation and also some thousand years earlier in the Hindu "Creation Hymn" of the *Rig-Veda*:

Then was not non-existent nor existent: there was no realm of air, no sky beyond it. What covered in, and where? And what gave shelter? Was water there, unfathomed depth of water? Death was not then, nor was there aught immortal: no Sign was there, the day's and night's divider. *That One Thing, breathless, breathed by its own nature*: Apart from it was nothing whatsoever.[8]

The emphasized section implies some kind of rhythmic process of moving between two poles symbolized as breathing. To use mathematical imagery, going from nothing to something is as if a point (one, timeless) becomes a line with an added dimension (time) capable of curving into a variety of shapes (creation of entities) singled out by intervals and peaks. This is the secret of rhythm in music, which thereby illuminates divine creation *with* time, involving permanence as a pattern of change, change *in* permanence.

In music the situation is more subtle than this for it is necessary to distinguish between meter and rhythm. "Meter" refers to the regular waves of strong and weak beats stated in the time signature (²⁄₄, ³⁄₄, ⁶⁄₈, etc.) at the beginning of notated music—what the conductor basically signifies to the orchestra. "Rhythm" rides over metrical waves and refers to the many patterns in pitch and duration of tones—it "is always rhythm-over-metre."[9] The very complexity and subtlety of these relationships may properly be thought to have an affinity with the complexity and subtlety of the overlapping interrelations that science has shown to exist in the created world.

Physical reality, especially as revealed by quantum mechanics and relativity theory, is furthermore characterized by its incompleteness of becoming and its pulsational character; the compatibility of the emergence of novelty with past causal influences; the individuality of events within the continuity of flux; the impossibility of instantaneous space and of simultaneous time and their replacement by that of "co-becoming." These are not readily visualized, so it is not surprising that a few other authors have also used the experience of music to conceptually model the imageless, dynamic patterns of the scientifically discovered nature of physical reality. For example, Alfred North Whitehead noted in his organic theory of the nature of the physical world that "a pattern need not endure in undifferentiated sameness through time. The pattern may be essentially one of aesthetic [that is, qualitative] contrasts requiring a lapse of time for its unfolding. *A tune is an example of such a pattern.* Thus the endurance of the pattern now means the reiteration of its successions of contrasts."[10]

In ordinary experience "movement" refers to progression through *space* at succeeding times, yet time has been the focus of our discussion so far because when one thinks of *moving* in music, one instinctively discerns the involvement of time. But what corresponds to *space* in music? It has been claimed that, just as visual icons have many dimensions of meaning and reference for Orthodox Christians, so "music attempting to be an icon may well be pan-dimensional."[11] Although rhythm clearly contributes to the sense of movement in music by characterizing particular points—or a succession of points—in time, other aspects of music perform equally determining roles: melody, often thought of as the *horizontal* dimension of music (even though it depends on pitch); harmony and counterpoint, correspondingly thought of as the *vertical* dimension; and timbre and texture (combinations of different timbres), almost another dimension. These attributes of music help us apprehend the balance of becoming and passing manifest in the evolving complexes of the natural world and so enrich our understanding of it as Creation.

The subtleties and complex possibilities in music are paralleled by those of the created order in another respect—reference to which has already occurred en passant—namely, that the moving patterns which come into existence with time have potentialities that are actualized only *in* time. To this we now move.

Second Movement

CREATION IN TIME

There is no marvel greater or more sublime than the rules of singing in harmony together in several parts, unknown to the ancients but at last discovered by man, the ape of his Creator; so that, through the skilful symphony of many voices, he should actually conjure up in a short part of an hour the vision of the world's total perpetuity in time; and that, in the sweetest sense of bliss enjoyed through Music, the echo of God, he should almost reach the contentment which God the Maker has in His Own works.

Johannes Kepler[1]

GENESIS FOR THE THIRD MILLENNIUM

There was God. And God was All-That-Was. God's Love overflowed and God said: "Let Other be. And let it have the capacity to become what it might be, making it make itself—and let it explore its potentialities."

And there was Other in God, a field of energy, vibrating energy—but no matter, space, time or form. Obeying its given laws and with one intensely hot surge of energy—a hot big bang—this Other exploded as the Universe from a point twelve or so billion years ago in our time, thereby making space.

Vibrating fundamental particles appeared, expanded and expanded, and cooled into clouds of gas, bathed in radiant light. Still the Universe went on expanding and condensing into swirling whirlpools of matter and light—a billion galaxies.

Five billion years ago, one star in one galaxy—our Sun—attracted round it matter as planets. One of them was our Earth. On Earth, the assembly of atoms and the temperature became just right to allow water and solid rock to form. Continents and mountains grew and in some deep wet crevice, or pool, or deep in the sea, just over three billion years ago some molecules became large and complex enough to make copies of themselves and became the first specks of life.

Life multiplied in the seas, diversifying and becoming more and more complex. Five hundred million years ago, creatures with solid skeletons—the vertebrates—appeared. Algae in the sea and green plants on land changed the atmosphere by making oxygen. Then three hundred million years ago, certain fish learned to crawl from the sea and live on the edge of land, breathing that oxygen from the air.

Now life burst into many forms—reptiles, mammals (and dinosaurs) on land—reptiles and birds in the air. Over millions of years the mammals began to develop complex brains that enabled them to learn. Among these were creatures who lived in trees. From these our first ancestors derived and then, only some sixty to eighty thousand years ago, the first men and women appeared. They began to know about themselves and what they were doing—they were not only conscious but also self-conscious. The first word, the first laugh was heard. The first paintings were made. The first sense of a destiny beyond—with the first signs of hope, for these people buried their dead with ritual. The first prayers were made to the One who made All-That-Is and All-That-Is-Becoming—the first experiences of goodness, beauty and truth—but also of their opposites, for human beings were free.[2]

From what we have seen so far it has become increasingly apparent that music can be a very rich resource for unraveling the subtle relation between divine creation and time, for music releases us from our mechanistic perception of physical time, the time marked by the clocks that dominate modern life. One only has to look at the accelerating processes of cosmic and biological evolution to realize that equal intervals of clock time do not have equal significance. Expositors of the world of science have frequently found that one needs, for example, a logarithmic scale to denote clearly the succession of various distinct stages in natural processes. Clock time does not provide an adequate metric. The same can be said also of the psychological experience of time, the rate of whose passage varies widely according to the content of what is being experienced. For all of us, time can "amble, trot, gallop and stand still" in "divers paces with divers persons."[3] Because time is its medium, music can show time as a basic aspect of reality in a way relevant to the processes both of creation and of our individual psychology. "Music is temporal art in the special sense that in it time reveals itself to experience."[4] Listening to music can reveal to us what time really is because musical time brings to expression experiential aspects of reality that physical (clock) time is unable to do. Victor Zuckerkandl has been especially percipient in making this contrast in the following way:[5]

Physical Time Concept	Musical Time Concept
Time is order, form of experience	Time is content of experience
Time measures events	Time produces events
Time is divisible into equal parts	Time knows no equality of parts
Time is perpetual transience	Time knows nothing of transience

The "musical time concept," as he calls it, clearly corresponds more closely to the characteristics of creation time, that is, to what has happened in the processes of cosmological and biological creation. Here we shall look more closely at the way in which musical time can illuminate our perception of these processes, for music is fundamentally involved with ordered changes of structure, with a flux that is not chaotic. It unfolds a temporal sequence and simultaneously reveals total patterns—both of which the scientist characteristically seeks in interpreting natural processes, seeing time as "the carrier or locus of innovative change."[6] Hence, as Jeremy Begbie urges, "music can be most theologically [and, we would add, scientifically] fruitful precisely in and through its ability to interact positively with time, and this is closely bound up with its thoroughly physical character."[7] What features of musical time might be significant for our perception of creation?

The Relation of Past, Present, and Future

In music the composer's intentions unfold in time, and the significance of any given moment is constituted both by what precedes it and by the way it forms a growth point for what follows. Past, present, and future interpenetrate each other: just as the scientist amalgamates natural sequences into one theoretical structure, so too the time sequence of musical experiences can often be apprehended in the memory as an organic complex. Yet particular notes, rhythms, harmonies, and dissonances—all that constitutes the music—have a different effect on the listener according to what has gone before. Each instantaneously experienced effect itself is the initiating point of its sequel, giving it a distinctive meaning. This is analogous to the way in which any meaning and significance we might wish to attribute to any given stage of the world's natural history is dependent both on what precedes and follows the point in question. Milic Capek, reflecting on the philosophical implications of modern physics, also sees in such features of physical reality, already referred to,[8] a parallel with this characteristic of music, which he suggests will offer a "key to the understanding of the nature of the type of 'extensive becoming' that seems to constitute the nature of physical reality."[9]

Let us consider a piece of music—for instance, a melody or, better, a polyphonic musical phrase. It is hardly necessary to underscore its successive character. As long as its movement is going on, it remains incomplete and in its successive unfolding we grasp in the most vivid and concrete way the incompleteness of every becoming. At each particular moment a new tone is added to the previous ones; more accurately, each new moment is constituted by the addition of a new musical quality. . . .

Every musical structure is by its own nature unfolding and incomplete; so is cosmic becoming, the time-space of modern physics. The musical structures, in virtue of their essentially temporal nature, cannot be subdivided ad infinitum without being destroyed. . . . For this reason musical wholes—like physical processes—are not infinitely divisible; in either case durationally instants are mere ideal limits, arbitrary cuts in the dynamic continuity of becoming. . . . In concrete temporal experience the emergence of novelty is possible, so to speak, only on the contrasting background of its immediate past; in a similar way a new musical qual-ity of the (provisionally) last tone acquires its individuality in contrast to, as well as in connection with, its antecedent musical context.[10]

At any instant, then, music leans toward the future, the basis of which is that, in a series of tones, each tone has a dynamic quality that signals incompleteness and points toward the next expected one. "Listening to music, then, we are not first in one tone, then in the next, and so forth. We are, rather, always *between* the tones, *on the way* from tone to tone; our hearing does not remain with the tone, it reaches through it and beyond it."[11]

Music and Creation as Process

This inbuilt anticipatory character of music raises an interesting question. Is a piece of music, say, a piano sonata by Ludwig van Beethoven, therefore played *toward* its closing cadences as if that were its goal? Surely not: what matters, what is intrinsi-cally valuable, is the experience of playing and listening to it as a whole. Although a given human work of musical composition attains a kind of finality in its closing cadence, it would be nonsense to suggest that the "meaning" of a musical work was to be found only there. Each instant, with its concurrent stored memory of the past as the ambience of the present and its ability to be forming the reaction to the mu-sic yet to be heard, has a significance that is sui generis and takes its meaning from its relation to the whole that is being gradually unfolded. The significance is in the *process* as such.

      This provides an important clue to how we should apprehend the presence of God in creation. Since coming into existence with time is intrinsic to creation, music helps us to understand creation through understanding time and its potentialities. Hence, it is appropriate that a model of the world as the music of the divine Creator-Composer also illuminates God's relation to the human listener to that music of creation as it unfolds in time. The model also properly includes the listener to a musical work, say, to that Beethoven sonata, and recognizes that there are times when one can be so deeply absorbed in it that for a moment one is actually thinking the music *with* the composer. In such moments we experience, in T. S. Elliot's words,

> music heard so deeply
> That it is not heard at all, but you are the music
> While the music lasts.[12]

Yet, if anyone were to ask at that moment "Where is Beethoven now?" one would have to reply that Beethoven-as-composer was to be found only in the music itself. The music would in some sense be Beethoven's inner musical thought kindled in us and we would genuinely be encountering Beethoven-as-composer. The whole experience is one of profound communication from composer to listener. This very closely models God's immanence in creation and God's self-communication in and through what God is creating. The processes revealed by the sciences are in themselves God acting as Creator so God is not to be found as some kind of extra factor added on to the processes of the world. God, to use language usually applied in sacramental theology, is in, with, and under all-that-is and all-that-goes-on. In reflecting profoundly on the worlds unveiled by the sciences we can indeed also experience in those moments the immanence of the transcendence of God as Creator of all-that-is. As scientific "listeners" to the music of creation, we encounter its Creator.

"Ends" in Music and Creation

Although the conclusion of a well-constructed musical composition is not its *goal*, nevertheless, when it does arrive the listener experiences a sense of completion and, in that sense, a consummation of the whole organic, complex growth of the work. In the Western tonal music that we are focusing on in this book such endings usually consist in well-recognized cadences in which a harmonic chord is followed by one based on the tonic key of that piece of music. Begbie has shrewdly pointed out that in some works the end is anticipated by the earlier occurrence of the concluding cadence.[13] He calls attention to such an anticipation of the end occurring quite early in the first movement of Beethoven's last string quartet, in which the concluding cadence is heard only ten bars from the beginning of the movement (CD track 3 at 0′23″ and 3′47″). A few moments later it occurs again and then at the end in an emphasizing musical context.

> So the movement *ends* three times with essentially the same cadential gesture . . . these closing gestures are woven into the musical argument and become integral to a rich and prolific development. There is . . . an interplay of the temporalities with an acute incongruence between the time of the "end" and the time in which there is a more straightforward unfolding of musical material. The two temporal continua collide, interact and are eventually woven together in the closing cadence.[14]

He argues convincingly that this expresses the capacity of historical time to anticipate consummatory events of spiritual significance, and he develops this in relation to Jesus' resurrection and the consummation of history in traditional Christian eschatology. Might this not also be applied to the processes of divine creation, especially to biological evolution in which crucial transitions occur whose significance is only fully realized in relation to wider wholes? Amphibians moving from water to land and breathing oxygen directly or the development of elementary brains and nervous systems are good examples of this application. Each stage has the appearance of a closure and the culmination of a long process, whereas, in a longer perspective, each stage is also the prefiguring of a later consummation in a more complex organism and environment. Again it is the *process* that is significant.

RESOLUTION OF TENSION AND REPETITION

Western tonal music generally involves a basic tonal structure that has been described as "equilibrium-tension-resolution," where "tension" refers to a wide range of musical situations that arouse a sense of anticipation and incompleteness, that something else must follow.[15] The means whereby this pattern is basically effected are, broadly speaking, rhythm and melody. As we mentioned earlier,[16] rhythm is always rhythm-over-meter and meter itself can be expressed in its patterns by changes in many aspects (or parameters) of music—pitch, harmony, texture (combination of sounds), new voices, volume of sound, and so on. Meter bears a complex relation to rhythm that "refers to the variegated pattern of durations given in a succession of tones."[17] Melody is a series of tones possessing a dynamic quality through the relation of the notes to the context of a "key," which is a series of notes proceeding upwards from a "tonic" note to form a scale (major or minor in most Western music, but not confined to these). Different combinations of the notes of such scales, because of their various kinds of interrelatedness, produce different kinds of harmonies and some sequences of these harmonies engender a sense of anticipation succeeded by closure and completion.

Begbie has illuminatingly related this basic musical feature, equilibrium-tension-resolution, to the narrative of creation-fall-redemption in the Christian tradition, with its future-directedness and concomitant need for patience in the face of delay and the incompleteness of the present.[18] In this perspective the processes of divine redemption are slow and often hardly discernible. In the context of this volume this is parallel to the slow, patient operation of divine creativity through the aeons of cosmic and biological evolution that have led to the emergence of sentient, self-conscious persons capable of a dynamic, personal, and fulfilling relation to their Creator. "A thousand years in thy sight are but as yesterday; when it is past or like a watch in the night" (Ps 90:4).

Musical processes, like natural ones, frequently involve repetition, sometimes exact but more often with subtle changes. Repetition within a piece of music, whether immediate or remote, does not lead to boredom for it always expresses a difference in sameness. "What is striking about music," however, "is that relations of sameness would appear to play a more crucial role than relations of difference."[19] Clearly, with no explicit external reality being denoted in music, repetition is essential for imprinting the shape of any section of music so that it can be recognized again and produce a sense of coherence and of intelligible form. What makes it interesting, and in some instances quite compelling, has been attributed to a combination of factors: that each repeat subtly alters some basic musical parameter; that each repeat is experienced as following or preceding different music from its earlier appearances; that each repeat occurs in relation to a different configuration of metrical tensions and resolutions—again that interrelatedness of past, present, and future so intrinsic to music. One of the most striking examples of this is the first movement of Beethoven's "Pastoral" Symphony no. 6 (CD track 4), in which in one passage almost the same rhythmic motif, linked with the same melody, is repeated forty-eight times without a break—only to be repeated again at a higher pitch.[20] Yet, it rivets our attention.

Over very long periods of time the processes of natural creation likewise establish what at first appear to be but a mere repetition of the form, say, of a biological organism.

But its context with other organisms, both predatory and symbiotic, and with climate and geology, can change so that its role in the ecosystem into which it is embedded is subtly modified. The possibilities of its own future evolution are thereby themselves modified over a longer period of time than is obvious in the shorter term when its stability is first noted by the biologist. Perhaps it is not, after all, surprising that the divinely created order can illuminate the way in which the Creator-Composer is at work.

TIME AS "VERY GOOD"

The first chapter of Genesis famously concludes with the judgment that "God saw everything that he had made and, indeed, it was very good" (v. 31). It has sometimes been deemed, however, that time—because of its ability to dissolve all humanly created physical and social structures—is contrary to all order and undermines all that is good and reestablishes chaos. Zuckerkandl strongly opposes "the dogma that order is possible only in the enduring, the immutably fixed, the substantial" and that music is "irreconcilable with order." For, he continues, "hearing music, we experience a time whose being is no longer a swift flare-up in the passage from one nonexistence to another nonexistence, which reveals itself rather as a self-storing and self-renewal than as a transience. . . . Order, liberated from all relation to things, pure order, bodiless, detached, and free, not as a mere concept, not as a dream, but as a vision beheld—it is to music that we owe our awareness that such a thing can exist."[21] In music, we experience ordered change that is *not* futile or inferior because it is transient, a dynamic process that can attain its perfection only through and by the passage of time. In music, time is therefore experienced as "very good" and assures us that, in spite of much to the contrary in our immediate experience, even short times can be fulfilling and creative. Music can reinforce the theological intuition that our limited span can be highly significant and life-enhancing for it can continuously bring forth new birth out of the death of dying notes, cadences, and sequences. Temporality is to be seen as a *good* gift of God, as expressed in Haydn's great choruses of *The Creation*—"The Heavens Are Telling" and "Achieved Is the Glorious Work" (CD track 5)—which depict the continuing, divinely created transformation of that primeval chaos that can still threaten our tranquillity and peace of mind. Time is intrinsic to the order created by God: our time and God's eternity are not irrevocably incommensurate. Both are held in existence within God's own Being.

Time as the Locus of Innovative Change— Moving Patterns with Potential

For a century or so now the scientific accounts of geology, biological evolution, and, more recently, cosmology have vindicated physicist Harold Schilling's description of time as "the carrier or locus of innovative change."[22] In and with time, atoms have emerged from quarks, molecules and macromolecules from atoms, living cells from self-copying macromolecules, organisms from cells, ecosystems from organisms. Similarly, notes engender melody, harmony, and timbre, which with time—through meter and rhythm—create musical forms. In a flight of fancy, Ursula Goodenough, a cell biologist, even writes:

> patterns of gene expression are to organisms as melodies and harmonies are to sonatas. It's all about which sets of proteins appear in a cell at the same time (the chords) and which sets come before or after other sets (the themes) and at what rate they appear (the tempos) and how they modulate one another (the developments and transitions). When these patterns go awry we may see malignancy. When they change by mutation we can get new kinds of organisms. When they work, we get a creature.[23]

The stages of growth of a living organism are the realization through interaction with its environment of the hidden potential implicit in its DNA.

Theme and Variations

Time in the created world unfolds the new, bringing out potentialities. Schilling's description of time can be pertinently applied to musical time since music can be a kind of metaphor both for the processes of the world and for our individual, qualified experiences, which are never uniform or constant but rather often patterned variations. In music new melodies and developments emerge intelligibly, yet inventively, out of earlier themes and fragments; and similarly in the processes of the world new forms develop from what precedes them, often surprisingly, though *post hoc* intelligibly in the light of the sciences. Composers often resort to creating variations on a theme. A popular and accessible example is Mozart's Piano Sonata in A Major (CD track 6). The delightful original theme is readily recognizable in the variations, even if the third one, *Alla Turca,* is somewhat exotic for Western ears. There are many and more subtle ways of transforming a theme. Thus the *Goldberg Variations* (CD track 7)—an essentially private work that Johann Sebastian Bach created for a harpsichordist to cheer the sleepless nights of his aristocratic employer—are based on the constancy of the fundamental, lower harmony of a sarabande (a form of dance) that Bach had earlier included in the notebook he made for his young wife, Anna Magdalena. One has to listen carefully to the bass in the deceptively simple first aria (the sarabande) for it is this, rather than the delightful upper tune itself that provides him in its simple, songlike symmetry with the opportunity to develop a wonderfully diverse set of variations before finally returning to the aria, now invested with a rich significance that could not have been anticipated at the outset. Is there not a parallel here with the instances in biological evolution when some less obvious characteristic of a living organism is the locus controlled by a mutation that becomes the launching pad, as it were, for crucial developments that help the organism to survive in new circumstances?

Fugues and Chance

It is now also clear from biological evolution and from work on complex systems that in the ongoing processes of the world new forms of both inorganic and living matter emerge by a combination of what we may designate as "chance" and "law." The inherent creativity of the natural processes of the world should be attributed to their mutual interplay. This raises a question for any theistic doctrine of creation: How is the assertion of God as Creator to be interpreted, indeed rendered intelligible, in the light of the interplay between random chance at various levels and "necessity"? This necessity arises from the very material stuff of the world having its particular "given" properties and lawlike behavior, which can be regarded as possessing potentialities that are written into Creation by the Creator's intention and purpose and are gradually actualized by the wide-ranging exploration that the operation of what we call "chance" makes possible.

It is here that the nature of musical creativity in composing a fugue is especially helpful as a model of God's creative activity. A fugue (from Latin *fuga,* "flight") is a musical form in which "three or more voices enter imitatively one after the other, each giving chase to the previous voice which 'flies' before it."[24] In a fugue simpler units are elaborated according to often conventional rules—lengthening or contracting notes, turning melodies upside down or back to front, squeezing different melodies together, playing different themes simultaneously—intermingled with much spontaneity, even episodic surprise. One of the supreme elaborations of this form is in Bach's *Well-Tempered Clavier,* which contains forty-eight preludes and fugues. The Fugue no. 2 in C Minor (CD track 8) illustrates some of the basic features of this form: a subject and counterpoint to the subject are played together at three levels ("voices"), interspersed with episodes using some of their motifs and moving between related keys before returning at the end to the tonic key.

If all this seems a little too cerebral for the twenty-first-century ear, listen to the last section of Benjamin Britten's *The Young Person's Guide to the Orchestra* (CD track 9), which begins with a broad, regal tune and successively gives it to the different instruments of the orchestra in various forms and then—in the last section, beginning with a fluttering of high piccolos—all the instruments join together in a fugue that combines each instrument's variation on the theme. Only in the last minute, in a blazing fanfare from the brass, does the original theme concurrently return and then fly on its way, competing with and combining what had been the piccolos' theme to make a joyous and exhilarating double fugue.

Executed with even more gusto is the great fugal chorus in which Giuseppe Verdi, in the last, masterly composition of his old age, has the character Falstaff leading the assembled company in Windsor Forest with his genial acceptance of his discomfiture ("The whole world's a jest") at the end of the opera that depicts his being outwitted by the "merry wives of Windsor" (CD track 10).

God as Creator "begins" with the fundamental divinely created properties of space-time-matter-energy, which, through their inherent potentialities in time, have become the diverse, complex, richly articulated world we observe today. As Creator, God might therefore be seen as a composer who, beginning with an arrangement of notes in an apparently simple subject, elaborates and expands it into new shapes—by a variety of devices of fragmentation, augmentation, and re-association; by turning it upside down and back to front; by overlapping these and other variations of it in a range of tonalities; by a profusion of sequences in time—always with the consequent interplay of sound flowing in an orderly way from the chosen initiating ploy. Time does indeed "fly" in a fugue. Thus does a composer like Bach create a complex, harmonious fusion of his seminal material, both through time and at any particular instant, that, beautiful in its elaboration, only reaches its consummation when, in the last few bars, all the threads have been drawn into the return to the tonic—the key of the initial melody whose potential elaboration was conceived from the moment it was first expounded. So God may be conceived of as aware of the potentialities of the order initially created in time that become actualized through those interlocking circumstances, appearing to us as random, what we call "chance."

The potential of the primal form of created order is known only to divine omniscience, but in the human sphere anticipation of musical creation is not so singular. One recalls how, on a May evening in 1747 at Frederick the Great's court, Bach was called upon by the king to improvise a three-part fugue on a theme supplied by the king himself, playing on one of the king's prized new "fortepianos." He did so and the king was suitably impressed. But Bach was not satisfied because not every subject is fit for such full development, so he chose a theme of his own and proceeded to improvise a *six*-part fugue—an extraordinary feat that, quite rightly, astonished the audience. As Douglas R. Hofstadter remarks, "one could probably liken the task of improvising a six-part fugue to the playing of sixty simultaneous blindfold games of chess, and winning them all."[25] This fugue, the "Ricercare a 6," became the centerpiece of *The Musical Offering* (CD track 11), subsequently dedicated to the king. Its various sections—a three-part fugue, ten canons, a trio sonata, as well as the six-part fugue—are all based on what Bach called his "royal theme." The subtle interweaving of quite simple motifs in this work is not unlike the dynamic complexity of, say, the human immune system, a network of interactions of specific large molecules, themselves constituted variably of simple building blocks.

A more modern model is the improvisation of a jazz virtuoso.[26] Introducing improvisation into this model of God as Composer incorporates the element of open adaptability, which any model of God's relation to a partly nondeterministic world should, however inadequately, represent.

When we listen to such musical "flying," whether composed or extemporized, we gain access, with the luxuriant and profuse growth that emanates from the original simple structure, to whole new worlds of emotional experience that are the result of the interplay between an expectation based on past experience ("law") and an openness to the new ("chance," in the sense that the listener cannot predict or control it). Thus might the Creator be imagined to unfold the God-given potentialities of the universe, nurturing by divine redemptive and providential actions those that are to come to fruition in the community of free beings—an Improviser of unsurpassed ingenuity. God appears to accomplish this unfolding by a process in which creative possibilities—inherent by divine intention within the fundamental entities of the universe and their interrelations—become actualized within a temporal development that is shaped and determined by those selfsame potentialities.

THE FULFILLING OF CREATION— CHRISTIAN THEMES

The Word/*Logos* produces a single melody—just as a musician tunes his lyre and skillfully combines the bass and the sharp notes, the middle and the others—holding the universe like a lyre, drawing together the things in air with those on earth, and those in the heaven with those in the air, and combines the whole with the parts, linking them with his command and will, and thus producing in beauty and harmony a single world and a single order within it. . . . The Word/Logos extends his power everywhere, illuminating all things visible and invisible, containing and enclosing them in himself, [giving] life and everything, everywhere, to each individually and to all together creating an exquisite single euphonious harmony.

    Augustine[1]

*T*he intuition we arrived at in the second movement, that the Creator unfolds the God-given potentialities of the universe, is given shape and form by traditional themes identified with a specifically Christian perspective. In that perspective, creation is consummated and fulfilled in the person of Jesus the Christ in whom God was experienced as uniquely present and embodied. These themes must, in our opinion, be reshaped to be in harmony with the new sounds emanating from the perspectives of the sciences on creation and on natural creative processes.[2] These re-shaped themes should inspire the Christian community to that working at creation expressed in the third movement of this work. So let us reflect on some of these re-shaped themes, which will form a bridge between the second and third movements of this book.

Some of the general themes, especially theological ones, that can be extracted from the subtly woven and ever-elaborating composition of the sciences that are concerned with humanity show, consistently with traditional Christian theology, that human beings are a part of nature, contingent, multilayered, and self-conscious persons that are ultimately mysterious in being "persons." Nevertheless, the sciences also point to themes dissonant with much of the Christian tradition as generally received, such as the following: human behavior has a partly genetic basis; human beings are a relatively recent arrival on Earth and in the universe; *biological* death is not so much the "wages of sin" as it is the means of creation through evolution; there has never existed a period of human perfection (moral or otherwise) from which there could have been a historical "fall." Such themes need to be incorporated into a transformed and richer harmonious unity.

More acutely than ever, these perspectives raise the paradox of a humanity that is a kind of misfit in its biological environment. Human beings possess self-consciousness which, by enabling them to be "subjects" over against "objects," renders them out of harmony with themselves, with each other, and with God—and therefore capable of, and actually, thwarting the divine purposes. Self-consciousness, by its very character as *self*-consciousness, has made human beings aware of what they might become—and of their failure to fulfill their potentialities and to satisfy their highest aspirations—and aware of personal death and human finitude, thereby enhancing suffering. Modern descriptions of the human state as "alienated," as possessing "false self-consciousness," and so on, all reflect a sense of incompleteness, a felt lack of integration and a widespread judgment that the life of human individuals today has failed to live up to the hopes engendered by scientific technology. These hopes have foundered on the rock of the obduracy of self-will operating in a humanity inadequate through its own inner paralysis of will to the challenge of its newly won knowledge and power over the world. Contributing crucially to this paralysis is the failure of humanity to discern what it should be becoming—that is, what it *ought* to be. No superficial palliatives can achieve the consummation of human potentialities and creativity—this necessary transformation would be that of the whole human being at the many levels of human existence in the individual and in society.

Significantly, in this context, experiences of a wide range of Western people, as recorded in many surveys, and the cumulative wisdom of the global religious traditions point together to a level of human cognition wherein human beings become aware of the existence of an all-encompassing Reality. This Reality, often called "God" in the equivalents of its various languages, transcends all yet is immanent in all existence, and relation to it appears to be essential for human survival and flourishing. In light of this, the religious experience of humanity is to be seen as constituted of a trial-and-error and conjecture-and-refutation process of interaction with that Reality, of encounter with God. Establishing such a relation would surely then be the basic condition for humanity to flourish both individually and as a species. For does not the human condition raise the profound question of what humanity's *true* environment really is? Thus it was that Augustine, after years of travail and even despair, addressed his Maker: "You have made us for yourself and our heart is restless till it rests in you."[3]

For humanity has to reckon with the nature of that Reality whose name is God, which has to be acknowledged in principle as greater than all else of which we can conceive and cannot, therefore, as the source and meaning of all-that-is, be less than personal. God seeks to convey to humanity both God's own meaning and God's own very self. So there is every reason to take with the utmost seriousness that long search by humanity for wisdom about its nature and true destiny, which is represented in the religious traditions. Moreover, if God is a self-communicating God who penetrates all-that-is, then we have to reckon with the outreach of God *to* humanity and the meanings *for* humanity that God is conveying. Acknowledging these two modes whereby the divine may be experienced and apprehended, when we ask the question, "What can *we* know of God's meaning for humanity in our Western culture?" we are compelled to recognize that—unique among the formative influences in *our* culture, and uniquely challenging in his person and teaching—there stands the figure of Jesus of Nazareth. The Christian proposition is that human beings have a potentiality, not yet realized, of being in the image and likeness of God, and that the figure of Jesus the Christ poses a basic initiative from God concerning the actualization of this potentiality.

In essence we suggest that the Christian affirmation is that God totally shaped the pattern of the identity of the human person of Jesus at all levels of his created humanity, and this was coincidental and coordinate with his total and personal human response of openness and obedience to God his "Father."[4] In this way, Jesus the Christ throws new light on the divine meaning of the multiple levels of the created world that were present in him—most of which came into existence through the evolution of the species Homo sapiens, to which he himself belonged. Implicit in our interpretation of this classical Christian theme is a strong emphasis on the physical embodiment of the Word (*Logos*), the self-expression, of God that parallels the embodiedness essential to musical improvisation, especially in jazz. The improviser has to think in the physicality of the notes and rhythms, has to indwell them so as to arrange them.[5] Creativity in jazz improvisation is holistically integral with movements and reactions of the body and models the unique integration of a divine and human spirit with a human body that is implicit in the Christian conviction that in Jesus the Christ the Word of God was "made flesh" (John 1:14 KJV).

The significance and potentiality of all levels of creation may be said to have been unfolded in Jesus the Christ. In his relation to God the Creator as a created human person, he mediates to us the *meaning* of creation—we learn through him that for which all things were made, how God has been shaping creation for the emergence of persons in communion with Godself. For the meaning that God communicates through Jesus the Christ, through the Christ-event, is the meaning of God both *about* humanity and *for* humanity. What Jesus discerns, proclaims, expresses, and reveals is the meaning that he, himself, *is*.

Jesus the Christ may then be seen as a unique focal point—though not necessarily an exclusive one—in which the diverse meanings written into the many levels of creation coalesce like rays of light with an intensity that so illuminates for us the purposes of God that we are better able to interpret God's meanings, communicated in his creative activity over a wider range of human experience of nature and history. This perception of "incarnation" is well expressed by theologian John Macquarrie: "Incarnation was not a sudden once-for-all-event . . . but is a process which began with the creation. . . . [It] is the progressive presencing and self-manifestation of the Logos [the self-expressive Word of God] in the physical and historical world. For the Christian, this process reaches its climax in Jesus Christ. . . . The difference between Christ and other agents of the Logos is one of degree, not of kind.[6]

This is an *inclusive* understanding of incarnation which allows and recognizes that the *Logos* of God is to be discerned in all cultures and all peoples, while recognizing the uniqueness of Jesus the Christ for Christians. Moreover, what Jesus the Christ was, and what happened to him, can, in this perspective, be seen as a new source and resource for reading God's meaning for humanity in all the levels of creation leading to and incorporated into humanity—the clue that points us to a meaning beyond itself, a key that unlocks the door onto a more ample vista, a focus of rays coming from many directions, and a characteristic gesture from the hand of God revealing God's meaning and purpose and nature.

How to express Jesus' integrity as a human person as least misleadingly as possible—while taking account of the presence in him of the ultimately transcendent God of love, which he revealed in his teaching, life, death, and resurrection—has been a perennial issue for Christians. Since 451 CE the Definition of the Church Council of Chalcedon has been taken as the criterion of orthodoxy concerning this baffling question of the relation of the two natures, divine and human, in the one person of Jesus. It affirmed that Jesus was "complete in regard to his humanity," that is, "completely human"—indeed, "perfect" in the sense of "complete"—fully human, but not necessarily displaying perfection in all conceivable human characteristics.[7] Any assessment of Jesus inevitably starts here, also recognizing his special vocation and relation to God. For the Definition implicitly points to the limits of our comprehension of the mysterious relation of the divine and human natures of Jesus by affirming that we should acknowledge "One and the Same Christ, Son, Lord, only-begotten made known in two natures, without confusion, without change, without division, without separation." The language of *substances* that is used here to model *natures* soon becomes incomprehensible—for one substance cannot occupy the same space as another and, in such a model, possession of the divine nature would seem to exclude that of the human, and vice versa. (That is why there has been pres-

sure to adopt more dynamic models whereby the human *activity* of Jesus is identified with divine *activity,* in accord with St. Paul's assertion that "in Christ God was
reconciling the world to himself" [2 Cor 5:19].)

It is in relation to imaging the presence of God in Jesus the Christ that a particular fundamental feature of music can be of help.[8] For in music we are accustomed to
hearing notes sounded *together* and we hear them in the one auditory "space" of our
consciousness through the cerebral, neural apparatus we have been endowed with
by evolution. Thus, if we are listening to one note and a second one is then played
that is in harmony with it, we hear a new, unique, *integrated* sound of a distinctive
kind, yet one in which the two separate sounds are still discernible. Both notes fill
the same auditory space without any exclusion of the other, but at the same time create a new musical experience—a chord. There is no question of the more of one, the
less of the other, for both together create the new synthesis and both are essential to
the experience of the chord.

The experience of a musical chord images the interpretation of Jesus the Christ
to which the experience of his first and later followers have been driven, namely,
that in his human person they encounter God. For Paul "God was in Christ." "Two
natures, without confusion, without change, without division, without separation,"
says Chalcedon more enigmatically. There is no question in the Christian experience of "the more of God, the less of the human Jesus," or vice versa, and this famil-
iar phenomenon in music serves to render intelligible, feasible, and credible what
otherwise would seem paradoxical, if not downright contradictory, as some critics
external to the Christian experience have claimed. In a work of music, the bringing together of particular notes into a distinctive chord can not only bring it to a
satisfying conclusion in a cadence but can also be the origin of new developments
not previously envisaged. For Christians, both of these aspects are operative in Jesus
the Christ because for them he is *both* the fulfillment in actual history of God's pur-

poses—gradually unfolded in the creative evolutionary process, and in the history of Israel—*and* the origin and assurance of new capacities for the individual human being and for human community, the works of the new creation of the Third Movement.

Polyphony, the sounding together of two or more relatively independent sequences of notes so that they interweave subtly (CD track 12) is closely related to harmony (the notes in the different lines have broadly to harmonize with each other as the melodies unfold). This parallels the way in which our physically rooted lives and earthly loves have to interweave with love for God.[9] Our resort to a musical interpretation of these Christian themes owes much to the work of Jeremy Begbie:

> Applied directly to the incarnation, polyphony highlights another and often forgotten feature of it, which . . . can be all too easily eclipsed by Chalcedon. The incarnation is not a theory, or a picture, or a concept—but essentially a drama of interpenetration between the triune God and humanity, extending from Bethlehem to Jerusalem, a story with shape, struggle and direction, and a glorious climax: Christ, as fully human, established in the life of God, humankind and God at last *together* as they were meant to be. Music can remind us that all the extraordinary patterns of interpenetration and resonance . . .—within God, between the Son and the humanity of Jesus, and between us and God—all participate in a magnificent multi-voiced symphony which has embraced dissonance at its most destructive, including the arresting dissonance and silence of Good Friday and Holy Saturday. Like all music, it is played out *for us* objectively in time, in the incarnate life of Christ, and now by virtue of the Spirit, it is played in and *through* us, catching us up in its manifold resonances.[10]

The need to incorporate dissonance could not be better illustrated than by the special poignancy and cogency, considering his imminent execution, in the reference made to these themes by theologian Dietrich Bonhoeffer in one of his prison letters, dated May 20, 1944, where he writes of the polyphony of the continuing God–humanity relation and of the incarnate divine–human nature of Jesus the Christ:

There is always a danger of intense love destroying what I might call the "polyphony" of life. What I mean is that God requires that we should love him eternally with our whole hearts, yet not so as to compromise or diminish our earthly affections, but as a kind of *cantus firmus*[11] to which the other melodies of life provide the counterpoint. Earthly affection is one these contrapuntal themes, a theme which enjoys an autonomy of its own. . . . Where the ground bass is firm and clear, there is nothing to stop the counterpoint from being developed to the utmost of its limits. Both ground bass and counterpoint are "without confusion and yet distinct," in the words of the Chalcedonian formula, like Christ in his divine and human natures. Perhaps the importance of polyphony in music lies in the fact that it is a musical reflection of this Christological truth, and that it is therefore an essential element in the Christian life.[12]

So far we have been turning to music to help us conceive of how two different entities can occupy one *space* and thereby illuminate what we can mean when we conceive of Jesus the Christ as God incarnate, as "two natures in one person." In the second movement, however, we reflected on how music can lead us to perceive *time* as "very good," for time, we said, "is intrinsic to the order created by God: our time and God's eternity are not irrevocably incommensurate."[13] This insight from music helps us to understand better the way the New Testament sees the temporal and the eternal to be mutually interpenetrating loci of each other, so that the events, in time, of the life, death, and resurrection of Jesus can be discerned also as manifestations of the Eternal, namely, God. Eternity is not to be reduced to time, nor time to eternity. Hence, designations of Jesus, whether contemporary with his life or the result of later reflection—*Christ* (Messiah, Anointed One), *Son of Man, Lord, Son of God, Logos* (Word)—constitute a web of metaphors expressing the reality of the historical, physical, spatiotemporal Jesus as the locus of the eternal, divine love. The process of affirming these together is given enhanced significance from our understanding of the nature of time in music.

The Divine Meaning for Human Becoming

Before we develop how working at creation in harmony with God's purposes can be illuminated by improvisation in the blues and, more generally, in jazz, we need to sound out more explicitly the Christian themes, the leitmotifs, as it were, of our third movement.

We earlier had to recognize the paradoxical character of our as yet unfinished humanity and our need to discern what we *ought* to be and *ought* to become. So we have now to ask: If God was in Christ, what does the Christ-event tell us about God's ultimate purposes for human nature, for human becoming—that is, for the realization of human potential, for human fulfillment, creativity, flourishing, and even consummation?

Jesus was distinctive in his openness to and intimacy with God his Father, in his complete self-offering obedience to the will of God to the point of his ultimate surrender to and acceptance of death by crucifixion, and in that the experience of his disciples caused them to believe that, after his very real death, his life—*his* particular life of *that* particular kind—had been taken in its full identity and personhood through death into the very Being of God in his resurrection. It was this belief that generated the conviction that he had an ultimate significance as a window into, an *ikon* of, God's own nature and that he revealed what humanity was meant by God to become—namely, united to God in self-offering love for God and others. Jesus' resurrection demonstrated to them, and now to us, that it is the union of *his* kind of life with God that is not broken by death and capable of being taken up into God. For he manifested the kind of human life that can fully become life with God not only here and now, but eternally, beyond the threshold of death. Hence, his imperative "Follow me" now constitutes for us a call for, and the manifestation of, the transformation of humanity into a new kind of human being and human becoming. Jesus saw clearly that what happened to him *could* happen to all. Humanity *can* be taken up into the life of God.

In this perspective Jesus the Christ, the whole Christ-event, has shown us what is possible for humanity. The actualization of this potentiality can properly be regarded as the consummation of the purposes of God in the evolution of humanity. To become one with God, to be fully open to God in self-offering love, is now to be perceived as the ultimate realization of human potential. Hence, Jesus the Christ occupies in spiritual history (that is, the history of the relationship of humanity with God) the place that a mutation does in biological evolution—an irreversible transformation into a new kind of existence allowing the actualization of new possibilities. In this sense, all humanity can aspire to becoming Christlike and can hope, as Paul puts it, to "take the shape/form of Christ" (Gal 4:19, NEB/REB) and this shape is cruciform. The incarnation was an act of new *creation* because the initiative was from God within human history, within the responsive human will of Jesus, inspired by that outreach of God into humanity traditionally designated as God the Holy Spirit. Jesus the Christ is thereby seen, in the context of the whole Christ-event, as the paradigm of what God intends for all human beings, now revealed as having the potentiality of responding to, being open to, and becoming one with God.

But how can what happened in and to Jesus there and then happen in us here and now? Can what happened in and to him be effectual, some two thousand years later, in a way that might actually enable us to live in harmony with God, ourselves, and our fellow human beings? That is, can we experience the fulfillment for which human nature yearns? How can what happened in and to Jesus the Christ actually evoke in us the response necessary for our reconciliation to God and so enable us to live in harmony with God and humanity here and now?

These questions may be answered effectively by seeing the life, suffering, and death of Jesus the Christ as an *act of love,* an act of love *of God,* an act of love *by God.* This "seeing" can take many forms in the manifold paths through life of human beings and in human culture. In the third movement we will try to gain insights through music into the consequences in our relations to other people of such a recognition of the love of God.

Christian thinking, as we have already seen, has been profoundly influenced by the opening of John's Gospel, where the divine *Logos* is affirmed as the self-expression of God in both creation and incarnation: "In the beginning was the Word and the Word was with God and the Word was God (1:1) . . . and the Word was made flesh and dwelt among us" (1:14 KJV). Let us pause for a moment and concentrate on this central event in human history, which is the seminal theme of the Christian faith: the death and resurrection of God incarnate as an expression of the divine love. Through the centuries, the representation of divine love has engaged the greatest creative geniuses of humanity in art, literature, and, our concern here, music. In this work, however, we have been concerned rather to see features of music as models and metaphors for aspects of creation—divine, natural, and human—and have not dipped into the vast reservoir of musical works that, through their very *con-*

tent, express Christian beliefs and experience. Nevertheless, at this bridging point of sketching specifically Christian themes as a prelude to the third movement, let us point to just two expressions of that pivotal, key moment (*Et incarnatus est,* "And was incarnate") in the Latin Mass, when, in the "Credo" ("I believe") section, the mystery of the incarnation of God in a human being is articulated in music.

Who can doubt that Beethoven, heterodox and unconventional believer that he certainly was, through his own experience of suffering surmounted by undaunted creativity, identified with the passion, death, and vindicating resurrection of Jesus as he wrote that sequence in the "Credo" (CD track 13) of his 1823 *Missa Solemnis?* Beginning with the almost boisterous allegro section (*Qui propter nos homines et propter nostrum salutem,* "Who for us humans and our salvation"), it enters then into the unearthly, mysterious adagio (*Et incarnatus est,* "And was incarnate" . . . *Et homo factus est,* "And was made man"), descends into the pain of death in the *adagio espressivo* section (*Crucifixus,* "Crucifixion"), and then triumphantly emerges in the *allegro molto* (*Et resurrexit,* "and rose").

Beethoven may have been inspired by the extant legend of Johann Sebastian Bach's masterpiece, the B Minor Mass, which was not published until 1845 or completely performed until 1859, more than a hundred years after Bach's death—for the then possessor of the manuscript (a certain Hans Georg Nägeli) had already in 1818 called it "the greatest musical artwork of all times and peoples." It was in the last few years of his life that Bach created his own work in this genre. It would seem that, on the threshold of old age, Bach wanted to leave behind timeless works when he died, a kind of monumental summary of his life's creativity in various musical spheres. He set about reassembling some of the finest music he had written in the previous decades, including *The Well-Tempered Clavier* (Book II), *The Musical Offering, The Art of Fugue,* and the *Goldberg Variations.* In the B Minor Mass he reworked, reshaped, refined, and integrated earlier works, but he did newly compose—possibly his very last vocal setting—the *Et incarnatus est* section. To listen to its quiet and reflective mysteriousness (CD track 14) is to prepare appropriately for the more extrovert and communal creativity evoked in our third movement—in working at creation and so extending the incarnation of the presence of God in the very stuff of existence.

Third Movement—*l'Envoi*

WORKING AT CREATION

THEME 1, THE BLUES: GRACE UNDER PRESSURE

An Ellington composition is the product of a musician who has an extraordinary embodiment, if not archetype, of the artist as playful improviser. It is in overall shape, and specific detail as well, the happy consequence of a very imaginative and highly skillful playfulness that achieves that measure of elegance that can take even the most functional activity to that special level of stylization known as fine art. . . . "C Jam Blues" . . . is also a perfect example of how Ellington used the jam session, which consists of an informal sequence of improvised choruses as the overall frame for a precisely controlled but still flexible instrument of composition.

What the basic message comes down to [is] grace under pressure, creativity in an emergency, [and] continuity in the face of disjuncture.[1]

Albert Murray

*T*he most famous two-note melody in jazz and blues might well be the opening riff, or jazz phrase, of the "C Jam Blues" by Duke Ellington (CD track 15). From these two notes springs a fountain of creative musical interpretations. As Albert Murray, a literary critic and social commentator, notes, Ellington's compositions are the embodiment of a "precisely controlled but still flexible instrument of composition."[2] Those two notes, and the twelve-bar blues structure, elicit rich and diverse musical improvisations. The blues can exemplify the very essence of God's creation and creative activity: diversity and unity, structure and novelty, ensemble and solo. God, the incomparable Improviser and Creator-Composer, takes the sheer givenness of our world and improvises on it with spirit and energy. God's ongoing creativity in the world is manifest in the implicit rationality and unfathomable beauty that both scientists and artists discern. Our world as creation, like the Ellington's "C Jam Blues," is an art form.

The blues, born and nurtured within the African American community, express struggles and hopes through a particular and powerful musical form. The power of the blues arises from repetition of the twelve-bar structure that undergirds and supports creative improvisations. The harmonic pattern permits "highly skillful playfulness." Structure supports the spirit of the improviser to embellish, to create anew. Never exactly the same, but recalling and remembering what went before (CD track 16). Contemporary blues artist, Keb' Mo' provides a superb example of this in his piece "The Perpetual Blues Machine." The overall framework of the blues results in a "precisely controlled but still flexible instrument composition."[3] God too is the playful Improviser, the musical artist who, along with the ensemble of creation, composes and plays measure after measure of elegant music. We join God, as co-improvisers, embellishing on God's theme of grace, freedom, and love for all creation.

The blues give voice to the stuff of life in all of its craziness, pain, and frustration. Each voice, each part, idiomatically sings its own tune. A scene in Toni Cade

Bambara's wonderful novel *The Salt Eaters,* written in an improvisational style, illustrates in literature what we are pursuing in music. Sitting on a stool in a hospital, Velma Henry, a young African American woman who has just attempted suicide, is addressed by Minnie Ransom, the local healer. Minnie urges Velma to face her pain and let it all out. She tells Velma to "sing the blues. . . . Growl all your want, sweetheart. I haven't heard a growl like that since Venus moved between the sun and the earth, mmmm, not since the coming of the Lord of the Flames. Yes, sweetheart, I haven't heard a good ole deep kneebend from-the-source such as that in some nineteen million years. Growl on."[4] God, like Minnie, listens to our groaning and growling, our singing of the blues. Even when words fail us, God's gracious love does not. In Minnie's words, God might say to us: "You gonna be all right . . . after awhile. It's all a matter of time. The law of time. And soon, sweetheart this will all be yours. You just hold that thought, ya hear?"[5] Velma must face her past experiences and also be open to what is new. God lets us know that we are going to be all right. All in good time. All in God's time.

God sings the blues with us, humming along with our words of pain and despair. But God's voice doesn't end there. If we listen we can hear God's Spirit transposing our notes of despair into a new key of hope. We live each day, each moment, as an improvisational prayer on God's theme of grace. With God's grace we learn to "perform under pressure"; we learn along the way. The blues reflect the way in which we turn the messiness of our lives into a fine art, improvising what seems like total chaos into a beautiful order. From moment to moment, in the daily hours of our lives, we learn: note by note, step by step, beat by beat. In the words of Jean-Pierre de Caussade, a seventeenth-century Jesuit: "We learn from experience for which Jesus came on earth to teach us. . . . And so we listen each moment to God in order to become learned in that divine theology which is founded on practice and experience."[6] We practice our faith. We listen again and again to the movements and moments of God's grace, learning how to perform with grace under pressure, to create art from the mundane. We learn by how we live, working out our salvation with fear and trembling, each day from beginning to end.

THEME 2, THE COLLABORATION: PRACTICE MAKES PERFECT

Let the same mind be in you that was in Christ Jesus,
    who, though he was in the form of God,
        did not regard equality with God
        as something to be exploited,
    but emptied himself,
        taking the form of a slave,
        being born in human likeness.
    And being found in human form,
        he humbled himself
        and became obedient to the point of death—
        even death on a cross.
    Therefore God also highly exalted him
        and gave him the name
        that is above every name,
    so that at the name of Jesus
        every knee should bend,
        in heaven and on earth and under the earth,
    and every tongue should confess
        that Jesus Christ is Lord,
        to the glory of God the Father.

Therefore, my beloved, just as you have always obeyed me, not only in my presence, but much more now in my absence, work out your own salvation with fear and trembling; for it is God who is at work in you, enabling you both to will and to work for his good pleasure.

Philippians 2:5-13

St. Paul draws on an early hymn of the church for his focus in his letter to the Philippians, which can shape the interpretation of how we "work out our salvation in fear and trembling." The working out of our salvation is a similar process to improvisation. The learning process involves the interplay of structure and freedom, repetition and dialogue, solo and ensemble. We learn the music of creation by practicing in an ensemble, with other voices learning their parts along with us. Biblical scholar Marcus Borg, in his book *The Heart of Christianity*, says: "Practice is about the living of the Christian way. And practice really should be thought of as plural. Practice is about practices, the means by which we live the Christian life."[7] We learn the way we practice, and the way we practice is the way we compose. When he wrote to his community as their spiritual guide, de Caussade remarked that faith "is like a musician who combines long practice with a perfect understanding of music, who is so immersed in his art that everything he undertakes connected with it will have a touch of this perfection."[8] Perfection is a process of understanding and immersion over time, practiced with others.

"Practicing the Christian faith" has become a catchphrase in recent Christian literature. Books on Christian living and practice line the shelves of bookstores. Whether from a commentary on the Benedictine Rule or in the writings of theologians like Dorothy Bass, the literature on how we practice our faith catches our attention. We may well wonder whether this is an encouraging note about interest in the Christian life or whether it is just another sign that our culture wants a quick fix for its spiritual malaise.

Why the renewed interest in the practice and discipline of the Christian faith? One reason is that when we practice a shared discipline with a specific goal in mind we develop shared worldviews and shared meanings together. According to Richard Rohr, a contemporary Roman Catholic theologian: "people are inherently sacramental. They know no other way to make sacred their lives except through ritual, song, symbol, prayer and holding human hands."[9] In a world that seems so fragmented and torn by violence and hatred, we crave togetherness marked by shared visions and shared times together. Yet, our lives reflect the isolation and fragmentation of our culture. We haul our children from one practice to another, we eat on the run, and then curl up at home in front of the television to tune out the craziness around us. But these practices are just encouraging more craziness, more fragmentation. We are overweight, bored, and out of shape. We are finding out that simply running is not enough. We crave quiet, peace within, time with each other. What is it that we need? What does our heart desire?

The church has not always met these needs. In fact, church bodies today reflect much of the same fragmentation and opposition as the cultural wars around them. We tire of simply fighting, separating ourselves with words that aim to hurt each other. We are looking for new ways to be church, to recompose our lives. We desire renewal. But we need a common vision that is more than just being like-minded, we need to be Christ-minded. What does this mean for us?

The issue about the ordination of homosexual persons is a crisis that threatens to divide many denominations. What does it mean to be church amid division? While we don't relish division or schism, we are not sure why a change in our "ensemble" should be so threatening. Both the substance of our faith and the form of our practice should be attentive to the times in which we live and to the good news of the gospel. We have kept the voices of certain groups of people—such as Jews, women, slaves, and children—from being heard. We silenced their music. What are we so afraid we are going to hear? We are rooted in a faith that sings the good news for all people. While the division in the years of the Reformation brought much chaos, it also brought about great changes, new ways of being church. Some churches try new music. Some think, "Maybe that will fix the frustration." So we create folk services, jazz services, and polka services—anything that seems to have a new beat. But we soon find out that the novelty wears off, leaving us empty again. Martin Luther, the great reformer of the sixteenth century, always reminded people that innovation was only for the sake of the gospel, to preach the good news. Innovation for its own sake was crippling. Tradition for its own sake was bondage to its past.

Change to our traditions would bring change to the composition of the music of our faith. Maybe we need a radically different metaphor, something to awaken us from our malaise and apathy. What if the ensemble of the church were modeled after a middle-school jazz band rehearsal? Odd? Maybe. Provocative? Yes. Instead of hoping we can always maintain a decorum that functions within rigid frameworks and beliefs, maybe we can let go into the dissonance, the clamor, and learn from it. After all, middle-school children seem to be chaotic, but underneath it all is a liveliness, energy, and enthusiasm about the music they are playing! But it will require letting go, both by the laity and by the clergy. We may have to relearn how to play the music!

How we compose the music depends on how we practice it. Learning how to improvise is like learning the language of the faith. And we practice the faith in the midst of our messy lives, amid suffering and joy, hope and despair, doubt and faith. So how do we compose our faith? Can we learn to improvise? To sing a new song? This requires different ways of being church, ways of taking risks together. The kind of church we become will reflect how we practice our faith, both individually and corporately.

When we learn how to improvise we learn how to practice. Learning a musical instrument and learning the language of the Christian faith are quite similar. Both come through practice. Both come through fingers, voice, memory, ears, and mind. Practice is about the body. And if we think about our model of a middle-school jazz band, we might discover that the bodies of middle-school children might not be so unlike the bodies in the Body of Christ. They are awkward, afraid of change, embarrassed to play the solo.

Many of us listen to jazz and blues and think that these great musicians just play on the spot, without any practice or preparation. They seem to make things up without any forethought. Their fingers seem to fly freely up and down the instrument. Their eyes hardly ever seem to be on the music but melt into the mood of the music. And yet our stereotype proves us wrong. Young children learning to improvise know how closely they have to look at the music; every note becomes their savior. They are terrified of letting go, of just playing the music for fun. Learning to improvise is much more complicated than simply making things up on the spot. This naive impression of jazz is about as realistic as thinking that learning a foreign language could be accomplished by osmosis and simply repeated in public conversation!

How we practice the music is how we learn the faith. Learning musical improvisation is indeed like learning to speak a new language. Neither learning to improvise nor speaking a language can be accomplished by the individual alone. By nature they are social processes; the group creates the setting for the individual's learning. Both are similar to learning a dance: responding to, attending to, and moving back and forth through the basic steps. At first the movement is awkward; feet may trip, the beat can't be felt. We concentrate so much on the step that we can't hear the music. But, like learning to dance, we learn to do so with partners. The environment should encourage and support the learner. Finally, the dance steps will come naturally. We might not even look at our feet anymore and simply enjoy the rhythm of the music.

Many of the great jazz and blues artists learned from other great artists, by playing together in informal jam sessions and sitting in with each other and sharing solos. From early on, music surrounded the artists. Whether jazz or classical, music was in the air. Learning happened through imitation and assimilation. Parents and teachers would encourage and support the young musician. Simply listening to the music, whether live or recorded, made the difference. Teaching and learning improvisation requires practice, playing, listening, and encouragement. Here are some steps toward learning a language or learning to improvise:

1. Listen, listen, listen to the genre or style: In jazz, listen for (a) a swing beat, (b) emphasis on notes between the beats, (c) dropped or "ghost" notes, (d) bent or blues notes, and (e) smooth, soft articulation. Listen, listen, and listen. Ideally, a new student should listen to the genre day and night, taking it into their eyes, minds, fingers, and feet.

2. Know the scales, the "alphabet" of the new language or style of music: (a) Know the scales so well that your fingers know them up and down, inside and out, in every rhythmic pattern imaginable; (b) learn several scales in several keys: major, minor, blues, modes, pentatonic. Build the alphabet, practice it. Sing it like you used to as a child ("A-B-C-D-E-F-G . . ."). Like scales, we learn many things in life them because we can sing them. We learn them when we can feel the tunes in our hands and feet. We have to trust our bodies: our fingers had to learn the way. Our bodies have a memory. They remember well how they have been treated, what they love, what they hate. Learning music is an incarnational experience, one felt deep in the flesh.

3. Create, borrow, and modify riffs: (a) Riffs are the words to the new jazz language—repeat them over and over until you hear them in your sleep. You really know you have learned a new language when you dream in that language. The language begins to haunt you, showing up in unexpected moments. (b) Use the

riffs as support for the soloist, listening carefully to what is "said." Soloists are only as good as the support they receive. The soloist must listen to the context, to the background support, otherwise the music is only a flourish, an embellishment. The context must give it meaning. (c) Then finally put the riffs together into musical phrases of one's own creation, back and forth, in all kinds of combinations. Practice will lead to something new.

4. After all the repetition and practice, you can begin to experiment a bit. Novelty doesn't come quickly. It builds on what has already been learned. Communication requires context, practice, and the ability to listen.

5. Listen again, imitate, model, experiment, and support. The roles go back and forth. One minute you are the soloist, eight bars later you are the support. Experimentation requires support and structure. You must know the tunes by heart and in your body. To adjust to different roles we must always listen. We begin by listening, and we finish by listening.

6. Dive in and don't be afraid. Wrong notes are not a sin. But notice that "dive in" is not the *first* step. Improvising is a process—one that moves through all the steps, all the time. The best musicians know this and they learn through practice. They are using the twelve-bar blues as a pattern for learning. Structure will provide freedom. We must begin with the basics—improvisation will come later. Like learning a language, the sounds and symbols are learned first, then the words, then phrases—then repetition, repetition, and more repetition. Only much later will actual exchanges between players occur.

So, what is improvisation? First and foremost, it is a process within an ensemble that empowers the individual and gives strength to the group. Improvisation is freedom within structure, individuality within collaboration, working and being in tune with others, developing the new language as native to one's self. Only then can the music really swing.

At the heart of the music of creation is the ongoing creativity of God and God's partners. Our calling in life is to create, to improvise on the themes of God's musical works. Learning how to improvise is practicing the music of the Christian faith. Like the beat and rhythm of music, God's movement is in, with, and under us. From early on in our faith we may sign ourselves with the cross, kneel at the altar, smell the incense, eat and drink, feel the water, or share the peace. Over and over, week after week, we bodily partake in the faith that we share.

For those of us who are from a liturgical tradition, we learn through the structure of worship. We move from invocation to benediction. And yet we must realize that the structure is there not simply for its own sake, but to proclaim the gospel of Jesus Christ. The gospel is about hope and that which is new in creation. Therefore, while the music of creation might build on traditional themes, it must also transform them. God's music must be learned and played in the world in which it is composed.

The liturgy, like the proclamation of the gospel, is an event, a process, an act. We begin with words, repeating them over and over. Many of us learned the creeds, prayers, and hymns at an early age. And someday when we are older, those words will come back to give solace and peace. They will live in our hearts and on our lips. When the minister says, "The Lord be with you," we will always know, "and also with you." This dialogue is created over years with God and self, with self and others, with the whole creation. The music of creation is an ensemble of voices and instruments that pray together, listening and responding.

THEME 3, THE ENSEMBLE: ONE BREAD, ONE BODY

For just as the body is one and has many members, and all the members of the body, though many, are one body, so it is with Christ. For in the one Spirit we were

all baptized into one body—Jews or Greeks, slaves or free—and we were all made
to drink of one Spirit.

     1 Corinthians 12:12

The church is the ensemble that composes and performs the musical works of the
new creation for God's future. The structure of the church can scarcely correspond
to the atmosphere in a middle-school jazz band, but we Christians worry far too
much about this structure and not enough about the process that comes from it.
We become obsessed with the *who* and *what* and not the *how*. But experts in family
systems remind us that family is defined not so much by structure as by function
and process. Might not the same be true of the family of God?

    Some research by systems and organizational theorists might be helpful for
thinking about the process and structure of the church. Michael Zack, a jazz musician who is also an organizational theorist, has offered his observations about the
structure and function of musical groups. Using an organizational theory framework, the following four types of improvisational music suggest not only the structure of the music but also the process and movement within the ensemble.[10] While
these four models offer provocative suggestions about the structure and tradition of
musical forms, we find that they must be amended to take into account our critiques
and concerns. For example, Zack's comments on the tradition of classical music do
not convey the elasticity and power of the performance of it. Therefore, we offer the
following:

1. *Classical*: The form and function of a classical symphony orchestra, while not
   the same as a jazz ensemble, which intentionally focuses more on improvisation, nonetheless elicits creativity and interpretation from the performers, the
   conductor, and the audience. While the music is already composed in its final-

ity, the musicians and the conductor offer their interpretation of the score and the audience participates in the power of the music as it listens. While the process of improvisation is shaped by the structure, it is certainly not determined by it (CD track 17, Ludwig van Beethoven's "Emperor" Concerto.

2. *Swing*: The music of great swing bands often provides the beginning point for students of improvisation. The vocabulary of the music is exchanged in patterns, creating a musical conversation that is scripted. Often, groups of instruments perform together as a solo voice. The jazz band leader gets the group going, maybe even playing along once in a while on an instrument. Give-and-take occurs within this somewhat more flexible ensemble (CD track 18, Duke Ellington's "Satin Doll").

3. *Bebop*: Bebop arose as a challenge to swing. The music demands a more complex structure in order to allow for deeper novelty and change. These musical conversations are more like those loosely structured around a meal where there is banter back and forth (CD track 19, Charlie Parker's "Moose the Mooche").

4. *Free Jazz*: From bebop comes free jazz, where everything is improvised—the structure, rules, content, and performance. For some people, listening to free jazz can be frustrating. It can sound like just a bunch of notes. But throughout the chaos is order and in the spontaneous back-and-forth there are meaningful exchanges, although the language might feel entirely new (CD track 20, Ornette Coleman's "Lonely Woman").

Zack's categories illustrate the movement and history of improvisation within different musical types. We can apply what we learn from them about music to what we observe about the form, history, and structure of the church, and also its process and movement. For example, during the Reformation, Luther shifted not only the structure of the church but also its process from hierarchy to the egalitarian priesthood of all believers, and from monologue to dialogue. In contemporary situations it is ironic that many of us who desire what is new are the most invested in maintaining things just the way they are. But when the "contemporary" service is as stagnant and rigid as the "traditional" service, all we have changed is the structure and not the process.

Luther's priesthood of all believers turned upside down the structure and process of the church during his lifetime. He gave voice to all, and made the vernacular the lyrics. To use theologian Larry Rasmussen's language, Luther used "creative deviance" to subvert the structure in order to maintain the power of the gospel.[11]

Calling on God's spirit to renew, to re-create, to recompose is risky. We never know where the Spirit of God might blow. The breath of God might blow a new life into people for the sake of the gospel, for the sake of the neighbor. We recall again our theme song, that Jesus "emptied himself, taking the form of a slave, being born in human likeness" (Philippians 2:7). When we sing the song of God, we do so in service to the neighbor. When we have the mind of Christ, when we share compassion and sympathy, we do so not for our own sake but always for the sake of serving the needs of people who are poor, voiceless, or who cannot sing their own song.

So we are called anew to co-create, to compose with God communities called "church" whose songs give voice to the voiceless, and hope to those who are downtrodden. We can think of the blues as the poetry of our song, the structure we build upon, and the way we practice our faith. The blues give voice to the complexity, messiness, pain, and hope of life. These practices bring about transformation, growth, and change within the music of creation and within the ensemble. God finds pleasure in us and who we are and what we do, in how we play the music. The music of creation accentuates both divine grace and human participation. Luther said, "God does not work in us without us; for He created and preserves us for this very purpose, that He might work in us and we might cooperate with Him, whether that occurs outside

His Kingdom, by His general omnipotence, or within His kingdom, by the special power of the Holy Spirit. . . . Thus he preaches, shows mercy to the poor, and comforts the afflicted by means of us."[12] We were created and preserved for this very purpose: to work with God. God delights in us and finds pleasure when those who are oppressed and miserable, the desperate and the damned, are lifted and made whole by our love and compassion. We work out our salvation, in cooperation with God, in order to enter into the flesh of others and bear others' burdens. And this is the theme of God's composition for creation: to perform with grace under pressure, to make what was mundane into art, to give life to the dead. What began in the exposition of God's creation will be recapitulated in the future. Behold, God will make all things new: "He will wipe every tear from their eyes. Death will be no more; mourning and crying and pain will be no more, for the first things have passed away" (Rev 20:4). The blues of our travail will melt into songs of hope. God will indeed make all things new. All things. That is the music, the music of all creation.

Coda

ONGOING CREATION

THE BRIGHT FIELD

I have seen the sun break through
to illuminate a small field
for a while, and gone my way
and forgotten it. But that was the pearl
of great price, the one field that had
treasure in it. I realize now
that I must give all that I have
to possess it. Life is not hurrying

on to a receding future, nor hankering after
an imagined past. It is turning
aside like Moses to the miracle

of the lit bush, to a brightness
that seemed as transitory as your youth
once, but is the eternity that awaits you.[1]
    R. S. Thomas

Then the Lord God formed man from the dust of the ground, and breathed into his
nostrils the breath of life; and the man became a living being.
    Genesis 2:7

That strain again! it had a dying fall . . .[2]
    William Shakespeare

According to the ancient Hebrew creation story, we are formed by God from the dust of the ground, and God breathes life into us. Knowing that our origins are from the dust of the ground, we also know the words, "we are dust and to dust we shall return" will probably be spoken when we die. We are finite creatures; God created us and all of creation with limits. The epic of evolution also tells us that from stardust we have been born and to the stars we shall return. Our beginnings and endings are wrapped in the dust of our finitude, our mortality.

While God does pronounce creation to be good, even very good, we know that we are finite creatures and that new life can only come from the death of the old. In a sense, from the minute we are born we are also dying. The creativity of the evolutionary process is built around this temporal process of life and death. No creature, including humans, can escape these limits. Reformed theologian Douglas John Hall explains this relationship between finitude and temporality: "Temporality . . . is of the essence of this creature's being—and not only temporality but the awareness of its temporality. . . . The human creature in God's intention is a finite creature, whose primary distinction from the other creatures is its knowledge of its finitude, and whose vocation is to accept and rejoice in this finitude."[3] While we may question whether we can rejoice in the limits of finitude, we can surely realize the necessity to accept and acknowledge our limitations.

Ecclesiastes reminds us: "For everything there is a season, and a time for every matter under heaven: a time to be born, and a time to die; a time to plant, and a time to pluck up what is planted" (Eccles 3:1-2). Death is unpredictable and sudden, coming too soon for some. For others, death lingers, slowly taking its time, moment by moment. Life is all a matter of timing, but we must realize that it is beyond our control. We come from dust and to dust we shall return. Our self-understanding as creatures born in a specific time and place is the center from which we began this reflection and it is the center to which we shall return. We can affirm Hall's notion that the Christian vocation is to acknowledge and accept our finitude and that only by facing our own death can we live fully in the grace of the present moment.

Many of us resist thinking about our own death. We read the obituaries in the paper, aware that others around us are dying, but we try to spare ourselves from the realization that we, too, are mortal. What we realize can be summarized by this quotation from Anglican theologian Jeremy Begbie: "Time is our destiny because our lives are lived in the knowledge that we are directed towards death. Time is, in a sense, our necessity, because there can be no un-knowing, re-living, or un-living."[4] As we think about our own death, we become acutely aware of how time passes. No sooner has an event occurred than it is lost. We fear this loss, the passing of the present into the past. What we hope for is more than the fifteen minutes of fame, a portrait of our life in Andy Warhol images. For everything there is a season, a time for everything under the sun. We live to die. And we die to live.

But our contemporary Western culture tells us that death is the enemy to be feared and avoided at all costs. Our life is geared to the future—to that which is bigger, better, faster. We are on a journey toward more and more. Our vocation, according to popular culture, is to be on the move. We seem unable to rest in the moment, to enjoy what we have. Time as we know it is mechanized and commodified. We are always on demand: e-mail at work, e-mail at home, voice mail on the cell phone, voice mail at work, voice mail at home. Sometimes the best vacation we can have is to just turn it all off. We live in a culture marked by time. Jay Griffiths, a contemporary author, in *A Sideways Look at Time,* comments that, "Looking at it once, it occurred to me that this is how modernity sees time; that we are so preoccupied with our gridded, subdivided constructions of numbered measurements that we lose sight of the gorgeous, lifeful thing itself. Modernity knows the strut and fret. But not the hour."[5] Some of us find our lives encapsulated by this conversation—someone passing in the hallway at work says, "Hi, how are you?" and you respond with, "I'm so tired," recalling all the events, commitments, and assignments yet to be completed. Throughout our life we move from one deadline to the next, wondering where the time went. Space and time are wed in a marriage rushed and arranged to accommodate our crazy lives. But what might happen if we viewed death not as the enemy, but as a natural part of our life, and the awareness of that death as something that actually might help us learn to live more fully in the present? Our challenge is to consider life from the perspective of those who are dying, whose every moment is precious to them, whose space and time are finite and fleeting. In listening to people who are dying we hear words of wisdom about living. Consider the comment of Annie Dillard: "Write as if you were dying. At the same time, assume you write for an audience consisting solely of terminal patients. That is, after all, the case. What would you begin writing if you knew that you would die soon? What could you say to a dying person that would not enrage by its triviality?"[6] What Dillard says about writing applies to living and dying, specifically to her question about how we face time. How do we live in the present when death is imminent? Ironically, that question applies not only to the terminally ill, but to all of us. Dillard suggests that we compose our life in the face of our death. How we compose our life is how we face our death. To consider Dillard's questions, we have chosen to listen to the sounds and silences of those who are dying. The music of their sounds and silence will be the metaphor to explore their compositions of life and death.

Music as an art form can convey all the depths and pathos of human experience. In *Theology and the Arts: Encountering God through Music, Art, and Rhetoric*, Richard Viladesau, a Roman Catholic theologian, claims that music has an intrinsic relationship to the sacred. To illustrate this he points to the way that Martin Luther understood the relationship between theology and music. For Martin Luther, music was second only to theology in conveying the Word of God. Viladesau notes that "Luther was extremely positive in his evaluation of music, 'except for theology there is no art that could be on the same level with music. . . .' In his view, music in the church served as a *predication sonora,* a resounding sermon. It was to be valued not only as a vehicle for sacred texts, but also as being in itself a mirror of God's beauty."[7] Music expresses what is difficult to express in words. Einojuhani Rautavaara, a Finnish composer, notes that there "exist different levels of knowledge, different truths, those that can be explained rationally and those that cannot be defined in words. Music is a language in which one can tell such truths ecstatically but without recourse to words."[8] Music serves as both a metaphor and method for conveying insights about the relationship of temporality and finitude from the perspective of those who are at the end of life.

Begbie's theological work speaks vividly to this relationship between finitude and time with helpful images and theological reflections: "My guiding conviction . . . is that music can serve to enrich and advance theology, extending our wisdom about God, God's relation to us and to the world at large. I hope to show this with particular attention to that dimension of the world we call time."[9] What is particularly powerful about Begbie's work is that, through the music, one can both think about and experience the images he creates. Theology becomes an aural experience. Music, as a temporal art form, helps the theologian generate new insights about the relationship between temporality, finitude, and the Creator.

One of Begbie's theological and musical interests is in a group of contemporary classical composers sometimes pejoratively known in the media as the "holy minimalists." What unites composers like John Tavener (Greek Orthodox), Arvo Pärt (Russian Orthodox), Henryk Górecki (Roman Catholic), and Einojuhani Rautavaara (Lutheran and Orthodox) is the way in which their explicit religious backgrounds affect their compositions. Their compositional techniques challenge and transform modern music, particularly its expression of temporality. In a commentary on the life of Arvo Pärt, Paul Hillier, a musician and writer, explains: "How we live depends on our relationship with death; how we make music depends on our relationship with silence."[10] What is fascinating about these composers is that their music, particularly the compositions of Pärt and Górecki, is requested by those who are dying. During the 1980s Pärt's music was played in a hospice for young men dying of AIDS. These young men referred to his *Tabula Rasa* as music of the angels.[11] Time, as experienced through the ears and hearts of those who are dying, is a guide for those who are living (CD track 21).

Our life, commingled of past, present, and future, presents itself as a spiritual and theological issue. Struggling between then and now, now and not yet, is simply part of being human. Pärt's music "obliterates the rigidities of space and time."[12] We live by dying. Humans are terminal beings. Yet, we seem unable to face this reality, a root of much of our spiritual malaise. As Begbie comments: "Human beings have always tried to control time by attempting to decelerate transience, to postpone the entropic process of decay. . . . Much of human history bears witness to the massive threat which death poses to all mortal, social and individual value, and the multitude of ways in which it becomes something to be held at bay, averted, cheated, controlled, or refused."[13] When we cannot face death, we cannot truly live. Consequently, we find every way possible to avoid death, to control our destiny, to avoid our limitations.

Some Christian theologians emphasize that "this time" and "this place" are only temporary and transient. We should be on a spiritual journey to another time and place that is more important; thus faith is what gets us to heaven (and away from earth). Contrary to this popular form of Christian piety, however, we learn from scripture that God resides in this time and space, and salvation is both now and not yet.[14] Paul Fiddes, a Baptist theologian, states that "salvation happens here and now. It is always in the present that God acts to heal and reconcile, entering into the disruption of human lives at great cost to himself, in order to share our predicament and to release us from it."[15] Creation, salvation, and new creation are a tripartite composition, ongoing, interwoven, sharing similar themes. The theme of creation resounds from beginning to end. What God intended in creation is carried out in the grace notes of new creation.

Our consumerist culture, like some Christian pieties, reinforces our sense of always being on the move, always running, looking ahead. Griffiths comments on modernity's attitude toward time and death: we have

a steep concern with the individual life, a hatred of aging and a reliance on professional expertise and medicalization. Moreover, they illustrate a refusal to join the cyclical aspect of death, so instead of being buried in earth, the body reabsorbed into a larger natural system, flesh to clay, they opt for an off-ground—and linear—event, the individual freezing herself or himself out of society, on a solo mission to escape the compost heap of communality of death by means of a fragmented individual "immortality." (This is symptomatic of the way modernity treats time, too; denying both its cyclic character and its earthy relationship to nature.)[16]

Our culture and popular religious pieties also reinforce the notion that time can be controlled and death denied. Yet, it is precisely the present moment, with all its rich depth, that those at the end of life dwell within and find their spiritual lives filled by. When death and finitude are accepted, then one is freed to live in the moment of God's grace. The present moment is transformed from a harried burden to a gracious place of rest. Time and space join in the grace of the present; they become a gift.

Begbie uses Pärt and others to reimagine and construct a different vision of time and finitude than that of either some Christian pieties or our modern culture. The music of the "holy minimalists" appeals to people fatigued by the pace of modernity. Rich Heffern, a Roman Catholic author, explains that the works of composers like Finland's Rautavaara, England's Tavener, Poland's Górecki, and Estonia's Pärt look "back to the roots of sacred music, combining the past with the present to anticipate the future.[17] Such composers meet a spiritual need. Viladesau notes how quickly their music has become widely accepted by so many different people:

A number of the best-known and widely respected composers of contemporary music are renowned largely for their explicitly religious works. Henryk Górecki notes that only a few years ago, no one paid any attention to his work; now, following the enormous success of his "Symphony of Sorrowful Songs" [CD track 22], whose lyrics include a prayer and a meditation on the sorrows of the Virgin Mary, he joins other religiously inspired composers such as Geoffrey Burgon, James Mc-Millan, John Tavener, and Arvo Pärt in forming one of the most creative forces of the late twentieth century.[18]

On first hearing their music, particularly that of Pärt and Górecki, one senses that something different from most Western music is happening. One is moved deeply by the pathos of the music through its stark and simple structures. Most striking is what is missing in other composition—silence. One learns to listen to the haunting silences between the sounds. Silence and sound then construct time in new ways.

The music of Pärt and Górecki is a critique of both modern and postmodern relationships to time. Begbie explains that "it may well be against this background that part of the current popularity of the music of Tavener (and perhaps Górecki and Pärt) can be understood—a counteractive to both modernism's tyranny of clock-time and postmodernism's fragmentation and multiplicity of times."[19] They do so by creating a temporal holy space that opens up the present moment. Begbie describes listening to their music as being like watching patterns of light slowly move on a wall. Much modern Western music proceeds with direction and development. The rhythm drives the composition forward, always on the move. "Sounds," Begbie states, "do not have to 'cut each other off' . . . or obscure each other, in the manner of visually perceived objects. . . . In the acoustic realm, in other words, there is no neat distinction between a place and its occupant."[20] Listeners find that space and time are joined together spatially, creating an opening in the present moment. The music offers an invitation to dwell fully in the present moment, to listen to silences and to sounds. The music rests, rejuvenates, and stays still in the present.

The music of these composers functions like resonant icons, transforming the present through the window of the divine. Madeleine L'Engle, in *Walking on Water,* explains the role of icons:

> The figure on the icon is not meant to represent literally what Peter or John or any of the apostles looked like, nor what Mary looked like, nor the child, Jesus . . . but it represents some *quality* of Jesus, or his mother, or his followers, and so becomes an open window through which we can be given a new glimpse of the love of God. Icons are painted with firm discipline, much prayer, and anonymity. In this way the iconographer is enabled to get out of the way, to listen, to serve the work.[21]

Through these musical windows we may glimpse the present moment. Like the liturgy that creates sacred time through rituals, this music changes and transforms time. The music itself becomes ritualistic. Hillier, in his biography of Pärt, explains: "The ritual aspect of this music derives both aesthetically and spiritually from its function as a sounding icon. The music ushers us into the presence of a recurring process: for ritual is not simply the repetition or re-enactment of structured events, but rather a return to the perennial condition."[22] Drawing on Orthodox notions of worship, Hillier explains that listening is an active response to God. Contemplation "is not a mere meditating upon things, but grasping them, dwelling in them."[23] In our musical listening, time not only sounds different, but also feels different—instead of moving forward, we experience the fullness of dwelling in the moment.

This difference is illustrated by exploring the relationship between *kairos* and *chronos,* two different experiences of time. L'Engle describes the difference: "Kairos. Real time. God's time. That time which breaks through chronos with a shock of joy, that time we do not recognize while we are experiencing it, but only afterwards, because kairos has nothing to do with chronological time. . . . 'The artist at work is in kairos. . . .' If we are to be aware of life while we are living it, we must have the courage to relinquish our hard-earned control of ourselves."[24] *Kairos* is the time signature of God's incarnational presence in our lives. God composes our lives through the artistic expression of *kairos,* a fullness of time. Time is experienced as qualitatively different, richer, and deeper. We experience *chronos* as the daily march of time in a forward direction, marked incrementally by timepieces. The difference between *kairos* and *chronos* may well be what we learn about the way dying people live in and with time.

This experience of the difference between *kairos* and *chronos* is beautifully illustrated in the writings of Christopher Bamford, a contemporary author. In "In the Presence of Death," Bamford writes about the way he experienced time as he watched the daily dying of his wife. Through this experience, he learned a different way of being in the world.

> Looking back, what seems most significant is the transformation that occurred in the experience of time. Everything slowed down, expanded, became qualitative, rather than quantitative. . . . Each day stretched out until it became like a whole life; and within that life the full presence of every moment was itself like a day. . . . In a word, with its routines and rituals, its different kinds of silences, the time surrounding her passing became rhythm. . . . Time became a set of Chinese boxes, in which each moment, each movement, contained others within others, life a fugue within a fugue, so that I thought if I could unpack one it would contain all. . . . Daily reality ceased to be linear and became more like a field within which relations, connections, emerged and disappeared, often several simultaneously. In that sense, time becomes space-like. Or rather, the experiences of time and space become so closely united that one could not separate them. Time became spatial, extended volumetric, dense, while space, that is, the sickroom and the phenomena

within it (the icons and flowers, the minerals and crystals, the vomit pail and the piles of papers and books and medicines, as well as the ever-changing light and air, the sounds and symphonic silences filled with insects, breezes, and scents) became temporal, a rhythmic dance.[25]

Reading Bamford is like listening to Pärt or Górecki. His words create for the reader the same kind of experience as a listener might have in experiencing the movement of time in a compositions like Pärt's or Górecki's. The music haunts the listener with broad, expansive forms that open and deepen the profound, expansive themes. Górecki's music, particularly his "Symphony of Sorrowful Songs," brings the laments of three different settings into spiritual focus. By allowing the music to build slowly and quietly into a resonant strength, Górecki engages the listener in the passion of the music, bodily. The suffering expressed through the soloist seeps slowly, like waters rising. But instead of experiencing a flood of emotions, one is quietly overwhelmed, submerged in the pathos of the music.

Listening to Pärt's *Tabula Rasa* is similar. Peter Phillips, contemporary commentator, writes the following about Pärt's compositional techniques:

> Pärt has developed a more articulated technique that he calls, "tintinnabuli." He likens it to the ringing of bells. It, too, revisits the technique of plainsong composition in its melodic contours, of which the most famous examples are contained in Pärt's Passio. Both Tavener and Pärt favor the use of drones (which guarantee a tonal, or even a modal, stability) and both like to repeat blocks of composition in a quasi-ritualistic way. Both tend to favor slow tempi.[26]

Much like liturgical rituals, the sacred becomes spatial and temporal. What is so striking about listening to *Tabula Rasa* (CD track 21) is the opening strike of the violins followed by a long silence. Then one hears more strings, the chimes follow, and silence again ensues. The violins seem ethereal. The chimes and solo violin strike a pace of beginnings and endings. The music is an odd arrangement of abrupt silence mixed with the stark beauty of the strings. The sounds of a clock bell striking with the violins, followed by silence, usher in another dimension to the way the time and space come together in the listener's experience. Time, as we know it from day to day, is transformed by this music. From the "strut and fret" emerges renewal and re-creation of the moment.

This liturgical experience of Tavener's and Pärt's music is reminiscent of worshiping at a Benedictine monastery. The relationship between silence and sound allows one to slow down, to listen to the presence of God. The steady chanting of the Psalms, interspersed with silences, punctuates the daily routine of Benedictine life. Hillier explains how this monastic experience can change and transform our lives:

> A monastery may be set apart from the temporal flow of ordinary events, yet the passage of time is none the less acutely observed, traditionally with bells marking the hours and summoning the fraternity to prayer at the appropriate time of day or night. Similarly, the year's cyclic processes are marked out and ritually observed according to the liturgical calendar, duly hallowed by force of repetition. This measuring of time within timelessness (like the bells run at sea to mark the track of time, where space stretches endlessly to the horizon's circle) provides the regulated motion, the matrix, in which the seed of the spiritual life can blossom.[27]

The quiet of a monastic community, the beauty of the setting, and the ritualized moments marked by worship help make graceful transitions in the daily experience of time and space.

In a way similar to the experience of rituals in monastic communities, those who are dying talk about the transformation of time and space when they listen to Pärt. Alex Ross, music critic for the *New Yorker,* has commented on why those who are terminally ill request the music of Pärt, particularly *Tabula Rasa*: "He has put his finger on something that is almost impossible to put into words—something to do with the power of music to obliterate the rigidities of space and time. One after the other, his chords silence the noise of the self, binding the mind to an eternal present."[28] In the experience of listening to Pärt's music, space and time interchange their qualities to become music of the moment; silence and sound, life and death are woven together into a cosmic, ritualized composition of God. Hillier explains that "It is possible that the fixed-state, non-narrative content of minimalist music serves the need for a sense of ritual. The use of repetitive patterns and harmonic stasis suggests an awareness of time quite different from the materiality of Western 'clock' time, though just as real to the person who experiences it."[29] The traditional drama of tension and resolution is missing in minimalist music, along with the relentless rhythmic drive forward. Like chanting the Psalms in a monastery, listening to *Tabula Rasa* is an example of the interchange of sound and silence. Pärt's use of drones reinforces the liturgical style of the composition.

How one hears will depend on how one listens to the silence. Bill McGlaughlin, Peabody Award–winning broadcaster and host of "Saint Paul Sunday Morning," explains this relationship between sound and silence in Pärt's compositional style: "What is interesting in Pärt's music is what is *not* there. There is little rhythmic complexity, no extravagant use of orchestration, no self-conscious harmonic display or dissonance. What we *do* find is a straightforward flowing rhythm, reminiscent of chant, and a very spare harmonic palette of pure intervals."[30]

What interests us is his use of intervals that create a sound much like a medieval chant. He sets up the perfect intervals (octave, fourth, fifth) together and in contrast to each other. They "have a miraculous effect. . . . The physicists can explain all of this in terms of mathematics: we're hearing overtones, they tell us. Angels or overtones? It doesn't matter. Arvo Pärt's simplicity touches us deeply."[31] The experience of this "angelic" music becomes ritualized, offering a different way of experiencing God's grace in the present moment. The fear of the future is transformed into the grace of living in the present. In acknowledging and facing their pending death, those who are at the end of their life are freed to live. We experience God in the way we listen to the silences in the composition of creation.

The way we live each moment is the way we compose our life. Dillard says, "What then shall I do with this morning? How we spend our days is, of course, how we spend our lives. What we do with this hour, and that one, is what we are doing."[32] Ritualized beginnings and endings give us the freedom to experience the power of the present. Bamford also notes the sense of time as liturgy: "Every day unfolded almost as a liturgy. So time also became liturgical, the enactment of a divine service in which not just I and the others around me but the whole universe participated with enormous love and reverence."[33]

Time, instead of a burden, becomes a gift. Bamford's experience of his wife's death is not only liturgical, but also deeply sacramental. Unlike the mechanized moments of daily ticking, checking Palm Pilots—watching the schedule—the movement of living and dying is liturgical with discrete beginnings and endings. Much like the experience of Benedictine spirituality, the movement of time is marked by beginnings and endings, by silence and sound. Ritualized moments open up the power of the present moment so that we can be fully present to God's gracious presence. God's gift to us is to live in the present tense. Just as Bamford realized, we become the living sacraments of the present moment to one and another. The practice of living and dying is our liturgical service to one another.

Many of us are often surprised at how full of life, how attentive to others and to the moment those who are dying can be. Those who are at the end of life teach all of us that life is not to be hoarded for self, but to be given back with joy and service to others. Their end of life becomes a ministry of presence for us. In dying we learn about living, and in living we learn about dying. We begin as we end. In dying to the moment, we learn how to live in the moment. We are born to die. Carpe diem. Yes, seize the day. This is the day that the Lord has made, rejoice and be glad in it. We only have this moment, God given.

Postlude

Except for theology [music] alone produces . . . a calm and joyful disposition. Manifest proof [of this is the fact] that the devil, the creator of saddening cares and disquieting worries, takes flight at the sound of music almost as he takes flight at the word of theology.[1]

Martin Luther

The virtuosity (or special calling) of a person is at the same time the melody of that person's life, and it means a simple, meager series of notes unless religion, with its endless rich variety, accompanies it with all notes and raises the simple song to a full-voiced, glorious harmony.[2]

Friedrich Schleiermacher

Music and theology, *sonorum verbum dei* ("the sound of the word of God"), have been brought together here in a composition about God's creation. Like improvising on a melody in jazz, our two voices riff on the themes of the Christian doctrine of creation from its beginnings to its endings. The voice of the scientist and theologian (Arthur Peacocke) reminds us that the final cadence or chord in a musical work is not the final goal of the piece. Yet, there is some kind of consummation, in medias res. The voice of the theologian and musician (Ann Pederson) reminds us that music is created in community, and this generates fruitful ways for understanding ecclesia as the people of God. Both of us can agree with Martin Luther that God's grace is experienced through the music of creation, as the grace notes in our lives. The postlude, a final piece played by the organ or other instruments, is part of the service of worship to God. Not to be simply used as "traveling" music, the postlude is the sending out of the people of God to be of service in the world: *Ite missa est* ("It is the dismissal, the sending out").

Glossary

adagio	a slow tempo
allegro	a fast, lively tempo
aria	a song of lyric quality for voice found in an opera or oratorio
arpeggio	a chord played with the notes separated
bebop	a complex jazz style from the 1940s
bent or blues notes	drop in pitch of select notes in the blues scale, sounding slurred.
cadence	a progression of chords that produces certain effects at the end of musical phrases
cantus firmus	a fixed melody played underneath other voices. *See also* n. 11, p. 105.
chord	simultaneous sounding of two or more notes
classical	a style of music composed in the late eighteenth century by composers like Mozart and Haydn
concerto	a large work for a solo instrument involving three to four movements and usually played with a symphonic orchestra

counterpoint, contrapuntal	two or more rhythmic and melodic voices sounding simultaneously
development	the second section of the sonata allegro form in which the main themes are expanded, broken up, and changed
dissonance	two or more notes when played together sound discordant in the main harmonic system of a particular piece
drone	sustained note performed in a piece, usually a bass note
dropped or "ghost" notes	in jazz or blues, a note intentionally sounding muffled or dropped
exposition	the initial theme or themes in the opening section of the sonata allegro form
forte	loud
fortissimo	very loud
free jazz	a form of jazz where the structure itself is improvised, pioneered by musicians like Ornette Coleman
fugue	a theme followed sequentially higher or lower in pitch by one or more other voices. *See also* the definition on p. 30.

grace note	a note that decorates a melodic line, usually printed in smaller type
interval	distance in pitch between two notes
jazz and blues	According to Langston Hughes, some say that the word *jazz* originated in New Orleans, others say it had an African origin. "Anyhow, by the time Louis Armstrong got to Chicago folks were calling all Dixieland bands jazz bands, and their new music was called jazz." The blues originated in the work songs and laments of the slaves, a "kind of musical cry." Eventually, jazz and the blues became icons of American music. (Langston Hughes, *The First Book of Jazz* [Hopewell, N.J.: Ecco Press, 1955], 38.)
key	the tonal center of a composition
leitmotif	a prominent musical theme that is linked to a certain person, emotion, or idea in the course of a work. Often associated with the works of Wagner.
mode	sets of scales that originally came from Greek music via the Middle Ages, and now used extensively in jazz and blues
modulation	change from one tonal center to another
motif/motives	a brief, recognizable melodic fragment or rhythmic pattern in a composition

oratorio	an extensive musical work based on a religious text that utilizes soloists, chorus, and orchestra, such as Handel's *Messiah*
pentatonic	a five-note scale
phrase	a musical sentence
pianissimo	very soft
plainsong	an unaccompanied vocal line sung like speech, often used in early sacred music
polyphony	two or more musical lines of relative independence
recapitulation	the restatement of the themes in the final section of the sonata allegro form
riff	a short rhythmic, melodic, or harmonic pattern repeated throughout a composition, usually used in jazz
sarabande	a slow dance in ¾ or 3⁄2 time that is usually part of a dance suite
scale	movement of notes up or down
sequence	musical phrase or phrase segment repeated at different intervals
swing	A style of American jazz characterized by the big band

swing beat	fundamental to jazz, the emphasis is on beats two and four, and the beat itself is subdivided unequally into long and short durations
symphony	a four-movement work composed for orchestra
tempo, tempi	time, the speed of the rhythm of a piece
theme	the main idea in a composition
time signature	the sign at the beginning of a piece indicating the number and kind of beats in a bar
tintinnabuli	the use of a triad to sound like bells (used in the work of Arvo Pärt)
tonic	the first degree of a scale or triad and often the home tone for a composition
twelve-bar blues	a chord progression that is repeated to form the harmonic foundation on which the music is improvised

Notes

Prelude

1. All quotations above taken from John Amis and Michael Rose, *Words about Music: An Anthology* (Boston: Faber & Faber, 1989), respectively.

2. See the following for Arthur Peacocke's previous discussions of this idea: *Creation and the World of Science: The Re-shaping of Belief,* 2d ed. (New York: Oxford University Press, 2004), 105–11; "The Theory of Relativity and Our World View," in *Einstein: The First Hundred Years,* ed. Maurice Goldsmith, Alan Mackay, and James Woudhuysen (New York: Pergamon Press, 1980), 87–89; *Intimations of Reality: Critical Realism in Science and Religion* (Notre Dame, Ind.: University of Notre Dame Press, 1984), 72–73; *Theology for a Scientific Age: Being and Becoming—Natural, Divine, and Human* (Minneapolis: Fortress Press, 1993), 41, 173–77, 205, 376; *From DNA to DEAN: Reflections and Explorations of a Priest-Scientist* (Norwich: Canterbury Press; Harrisburg, Pa.: Distributed in the U.S. by Morehouse, 1996), 44–46, 75; *Paths from Science towards God: The End of All Our Exploring* (Oxford: Oneworld, 2001), 77–78, 137–38.

3. See the following for Ann Pederson's previous work: *Where in the World Is God? Variations on a Theme* (St. Louis: Chalice Press, 1998), and *God, Creation, and All That Jazz: A Process of Composition and Improvisation* (St. Louis: Chalice Press, 2001).

First Movement

1. Thomas Traherne, *Centuries* (London: Faith Press, 1960 [1670]) 3,3.

2. Proposals include quantum fluctuations in a quantum field (which is certainly not "nothing" even if not a "thing"), giving rise to matter-energy; superstring and M-theories that

postulate filaments whose vibrations give rise to what were previously thought of as "elementary" particles and that require, respectively, ten or eleven dimensions that *include* the usual four: three of space and one of time (see Brian Greene, *The Fabric of the Cosmos: Space, Time, and the Texture of Reality* [New York: Knopf, 2004]; and the distinction between time and space breaking down in or around the singularity (see Steven Hawking, *A Brief History of Time: From the Big Bang to Black Holes* [New York: Bantam Books, 1988]).

3. See Arthur Peacocke, *Paths from Science towards God: The End of All Our Exploring* (Oxford: Oneworld, 2001), chaps. 3–7.

4. Lewis Carroll, *Alice through the Looking Glass* (New York: Nonesuch Press, 1939), 172–74.

5. Augustine, *Confessions* XI, 10, trans. R. S. Pine-Coffin (New York: Penguin Putnam, 1961), 262–63, 279.

6. C. S. Lewis, *The Magician's Nephew,* illus. Pauline Baynes (London: Bodley Head, 1955), 93–94.

7. Karl Popper, *The Unended Quest: An Intellectual Autobiography,* rev. ed. (London: Fontana, 1976), 59.

8. "Creation Hymn" of the *Rig-Veda,* in *The Pocket World Bible,* ed. R. O. Ballou (London: Routledge, 1948), 30, emphasis added.

9. Jeremy S. Begbie, *Theology, Music, and Time* (New York: Cambridge University Press, 2000), 41.

10. Alfred North Whitehead, *Science and the Modern World* (New York: Macmillan, 1925), 193, emphasis added.

11. Ivan Moody, "Icons in Music? Two Works by Tavener," *Sobornost* 1 (March 1988): 37.

Second Movement

1. In the translation of Karl Popper, *The Unended Quest: An Intellectual Autobiography,* rev.

ed. (London: Fontana, 1976), 59, based on the Latin text of D. Perrkin Walker, "Kepler's Celestial Music," *J. Warburg and Courtauld Institute* 30 (1967): 249, taken from Johannes Kepler, *Gesammelte Werke,* vol. 6, ed. Max Caspar (Munich: C. H. Beck, 1940), 328.

2. Arthur Peacocke, *Paths from Science towards God: The End of All Our Exploring* (Oxford: Oneworld, 2001), 1–2.

3. Rosalind, in *As You Like It,* act 3, scene 2, lines 301–4 (William Shakespeare, *Complete Works* [Oxford: Clarendon Press, 1988]).

4. Victor Zuckerkandl, *Sound and Symbol,* trans. Willard R. Trask and Norbert Guterman (New York: Pantheon, 1956), 200.

5. Ibid., 202.

6. Harold K. Schilling, *The New Consciousness in Science and Religion* (London: SCM Press, 1973), 126.

7. Jeremy S. Begbie, "Theology and Music in the Arts," in *The Modern Theologians: An Introduction to Christian Theology in the Twentieth Century,* 2d ed. ed. David F. Ford (Cambridge, Mass.: Blackwell, 1997), 688.

8. See page 14 above.

9. Milic Capek, *The Philosophical Impact of Contemporary Physics* (Princeton, N.J.: Van Nostrand, 1961), 399.

10. Ibid., 371–73.

11. Zuckerkandl, *Sound and Symbol,* 136–37.

12. T. S. Eliot "The Dry Salvages," in *The Four Quartets* (London: Faber & Faber, 1944), lines 210–12.

13. Jeremy S. Begbie, *Theology, Music, and Time* (New York: Cambridge University Press, 2000), 111–18.

14. Ibid., 116.

15. See Begbie, *Theology, Music, and Time,* chap. 4, for the musicological literature relevant to this statement

16. See page 14 above.

17. Begbie, *Theology, Music, and Time,* 41. The comments here depend on the exposition in his chapter 2, "Music's Time."

18. Ibid., chap. 4, "Resolution and Salvation."

19. Ibid., 156, and chap. 6, "Repetition and Eucharist."

20. Ibid.

21. Zuckerkandl, *Sound and Symbol,* 241.

22. H. K. Schilling, *The New Consciousness in Science and Religion* (London: SCM Press, 1973), 126.

23. Ursula Goodenough, *The Sacred Depths of Nature* (New York: Oxford University Press, 1998), 58–59.

24. *The New Oxford Companion to Music* (New York: Oxford University Press, 1983), s.v. "fugue."

25. Douglas R. Hofstadter, *Gödel, Escher, Bach: An Eternal Golden Braid* (New York: Basic Books, 1979), 7.

26. See the third movement in this book for our discussion of jazz improvisation as a model for divine creativity.

Bridge Passage

1. Adapted by the authors from Augustine, *Contra Gentiles* and *De Incarnatione,* ed. and trans. R. W. Thomson (Oxford: Clarendon Press, 1971).

2. For a brief account of such a "transforming," see Arthur R. Peacocke, *God and Science: A Quest for Christian Credibility* (London: SCM Press, 1996). The present text reflects parts of chapters 3 and 4 of that work, "Human Being" and "Divine Meaning and Human Becoming," respectively.

3. Augustine, *Confessions,* X, 1, trans. R. S. Pine-Coffin (New York: Penguin Putnam, 1961), 1.

4. "*Informing* is the more technical word for this shaping of the pattern of the identity of his person. See Arthur R. Peacocke, "The Incarnation of the Informing Self-Expressive Word of God," in *Religion and Science: History, Method, Dialogue,* ed. W. Mark Richardson and Wesley J. Wildman (New York: Routledge, 1996), 321–39; reprinted in *Evolution: The Disguised Friend of Faith?* (Radnor, Pa.: Templeton Foundation Press, 2004), chap. 10.

5. See the third movement in this book for our discussion of jazz improvisation as a model for divine creativity.

6. John Macquarrie, *Jesus Christ in Modern Thought* (Philadelphia: Trinity Press International, 1990), 392.

7. John A. T. Robinson, *The Human Face of God* (London: SCM Press, 1973), 68 and n3.

8. Colin E. Gunton, *Yesterday and Today: A Study of Continuities in Christology* (Grand Rapids, MI: Eerdmans, 1983), 115 ff.; and Jeremy Begbie, ed., "Through Music: Sound Mix," in *Beholding the Glory: Incarnation through the Arts* (Grand Rapids, Mich.: Baker Books, 2000), 141–47.

9. An idea to be developed in the third movement.

10. Begbie, *Beholding the Glory*, 150–51.

11. Usually, a *cantus firmus* is a "pre-existing melody taken as the basis of a new polyphonic composition . . . usually 'held' in long notes in the lower voice" (*The New Oxford Companion to Music* [New York: Oxford University Press, 1983], 312).

12. Dietrich Bonhoeffer, *Letters and Papers from Prison* (London: Fontana, 1959), 99–100.

13. See p. 28.

Third Movement

1. Albert Murray, *The Blue Devils of Nada: A Contemporary American Approach to Aesthetic Statement* (New York: Vintage Books, 1996), 107, 94–95.

2. Ibid., 107.

3. Ibid.

4. Toni Cade Bambara, *The Salt Eaters* (New York: Vintage Books, 1980), 41.

5. Ibid.

6. Jean-Pierre de Caussade, *The Sacrament of the Present Moment*, trans. Kitty Muggeridge (San Francisco: Harper & Row, 1996), 88.

7. Marcus J. Borg, *The Heart of Christianity: Rediscovering a Life of Faith* (San Francisco: HarperSanFrancisco, 2003), 187.

8. de Caussade, *The Sacrament of the Present Moment*, 55.

9. Richard Rohr, *National Catholic Reporter* 38, no. 16 (February 22, 2002): 3.

10. Michael H. Zack, "Jazz Improvisation and Organizing: Once More from the Top," *Organizational Science* 11, no. 2 (March–April 2000): 227–336.

11. Larry Rasmussen, "Shaping Communities," in *Practicing Our Faith*, ed. Dorothy C. Bass (San Francisco: Jossey-Bass Publishers, 1997), 125.

12. Martin Luther, *The Bondage of the Will*, trans. J. I. Packer and O. R. Johnston (London: James Clarke, 1957), 268.

Coda

1. R. S. Thomas, *Later Poems: A Selection 1972–1982* (London: Macmillan, 1983), 81.

2. Orsino, in William Shakespeare's *Twelfth Night*, act 1, scene 1, line 4 in, *Complete Works* (Oxford: Clarendon Press, 1988).

3. Douglas John Hall, *God and Human Suffering: An Exercise in the Theology of the Cross* (Minneapolis: Augsburg Publishing House, 1986), 80.

4. Jeremy S. Begbie, *Theology, Music, and Time* (New York: Cambridge University Press, 2000), 30.

5. Jay Griffiths, *A Sideways Look at Time* (New York: Putnam, 2002), 1.

6. Annie Dillard, *The Writing Life* (New York: Harper & Row, 1989), 68.

7. Richard Viladesau, *Theology and the Arts: Encountering God through Music, Art, and Rhetoric* (New York: Paulist Press, 2000), 25–26.

8. Rich Heffern, "Spirit in Sound: New Sacred Music with Beauty as a Medium, Composers Echo the Beating Heart of God," *National Catholic Reporter* 39, no. 7 (December 13, 2002): 6

9. Begbie, *Theology, Music, and Time,* 3.

10. Paul Hillier, *Arvo Pärt* (New York: Oxford University Press, 1997), 1.

11. Patrick Giles, "Arts and Entertainment Review: Sharps and Flats," *Salon,* November 18, 1999, http://archive.salon.com/ent/music/review/1999/11/18/tabula/.

12. Alex Ross, "Consolations," *New Yorker* 78, no. 37 (December 2, 2002): 114.

13. Begbie, *Theology, Music, and Time,* 72.

14. "Now after John was arrested, Jesus came to Galilee, proclaiming the good news of God, and saying, 'The time is fulfilled, and the kingdom of God has come near; repent, and believe in the good news," (Mark 1:14-15).

15. Paul Fiddes, *Past Event and Present Salvation: The Christian Idea of Atonement* (Louisville, Ky.: Westminster John Knox Press, 1989), 14.

16. Griffiths, *A Sideways Look at Time,* 321.

17. Heffern, "Spirit in Sound," 1.

18. Viladesau, *Theology and the* Arts, 11.

19. Begbie, *Theology, Music, and Time,* 74.

20. Ibid., 24.

21. Madeleine L'Engle, *Walking on Water: Reflections on Faith and Art* (Wheaton, Ill.: Harold Shaw Publishers, 1980), 28.

22. Hillier, *Arvo Pärt,* 17–18.

23. Ibid., 16.

24. L'Engle, *Walking on Water,* 98–99.

25. Christopher Bamford, "In the Presence of Death," in *The Best Spiritual Writing 2000,* ed. Philip Zaleski (San Francisco: HarperSanFrancisco, 2000), 3.

26. Peter Phillips, review of *Arvo Pärt,* by Peter Hillier, in the *New Republic* 217, no. 22 (December 1, 1997): 2.

27. Hillier, *Arvo Pärt,* 192.

28. Ross, "Consolations," 110.

29. Hillier, *Arvo Pärt,* 17.

30. Bill McGlaughlin, "Arvo Pärt and the New Simplicity," *Saint Paul Sunday,* October 11, 1998, http://saintpaulsunday.publicradio.org/features/9810_part/index.htm.

31. Ibid.

32. Dillard, *The Writing Life,* 32.

33. Bamford, "In the Presence of Death," 4.

Postlude

1. In a letter to Louis Senfl during Luther's time in prison, dated Coburg, October 4, 1530. From *Luther's Works: American Edition*, vol. 49 (Philadelphia: Fortress Press, 1972), 428.

2. Friedrich Schleiermacher quoted in Jaroslav Pelikan, *The Melody of Theology: A Philosophical Dictionary* (Cambridge: Harvard University Press, 1988), 167.

Index

adagio, defined, 83
allegro, defined, 83
arias, defined, 83
arpeggio, defined, 83
Augustine, Saint, 8–9, 37–38

Bach, Anna Magdalena, 29
Bach, Johann Sebastian, 29, 30–32, 47–48
Bambara, Toni Cade, 50–51
Bamford, Christopher, 75–76, 79–80
Bass, Dorothy, 53
bebop, 61
    defined, 83
Beethoven, Ludwig von, 22–23, 24, 26, 47, 61
Begbie, Jeremy, 20, 24, 25, 42, 67, 70–72
Benedictine Rule, 53
bent notes, defined, 83
Big Bang Theory. *See* Hot Big Bang
biological evolution. *See* evolution
blues
    defined, 85
    as grace under pressure, 49–52
    improvisation, 44, 57–58

notes, defined, 83
    twelve-bar, defined, 87
Bonhoeffer, Dietrich, 43
Borg, Marcus, 53
Brecht, Berthold, 1–2
Britten, Benjamin, 31
Browne, Thomas, 1
Burgon, Geoffrey, 73

Cadences, defined, 83
cantus firmus, 43
    defined, 83, 93 n.11
Capek, Milic, 21–22
Carroll, Lewis, 7–8
Caussade, Jean-Pierre de, 51
chance, 30–33
change and time, 28–33
chaos, 27–28
chords
    defined, 83
    synthesis of, 41
Christianity
    on creation, 7, 35–48, 81
    on human beings, 36–38

CD Track List

The authors gratefully acknowledge permissions to reproduce and distribute the following recordings.

1. Franz Joseph Haydn, *The Creation*, "The Representation of Chaos"
   From *The Creation*, Johannes Somary, Fairfield County Chorale, Newport Classic NPD085627 Produced under license from Newport Classic, Ltd. 11 Willow St. Newport, RI 02840 Newportclassic.com.

2. Richard Wagner, Prelude to *Das Rheingold*
   From *Richard Wagner, Der Ring des Nibelungen*, Bayreuth 1956. Hans Knappertsbush. (p) Music and Arts Programs of America. CD-4009 (13).

3. Ludwig van Beethoven, String Quartet in F Major, op. 135
   From *Beethoven—The Late Quartets*. The Busch Quartet. Pearl Pavilion Records. Courtesy of Pavilion Records from GEM 0053.

4. Ludwig van Beethoven, Symphony no. 6 in F Major (the "Pastoral" Symphony)
   From *Otto Klemperer in Concert: Beethoven Symphonies No. 6 in F and No. 8*. Amsterdam Concertgebouw 1956/57. (p) Music and Arts Programs of America, Inc. CD-246.

5. Franz Joseph Haydn, *The Creation*, Achieved is the glorious work/Our song must be the praise of God/Glory to his Name for ever/He sole on high exalted reigns
   From *The Creation*, Johannes Somary, Fairfield County Chorale, Newport Classic NPD085627 Produced under license from Newport Classic, Ltd. 11 Willow St. Newport, RI 02840 Newportclassic.com.

6. Wolfgang Amadeus Mozart, Piano Sonata in A Major, K. 331 (the theme and the first three variations)
   From *Solomon Testament: Mozart: Piano Sonatas Nos. 11 & 17*. (p) EMI Records SBT 1221.

7.   Johann Sebastian Bach, *Goldberg Variations* (the aria and the first three variations)
     From *Bach—Goldberg Variations*. Anthony Newman, Harpsichord. Sony Music. QK
     62582. Courtesy of Sony BMG Music Entertainment.

8.   Johann Sebastian Bach, *The Well-Tempered Clavier*, Book 1, Fugue no. 2 in C Minor
     From *Bach—The Well-Tempered Clavier*, Book 1. Angela Hewitt, piano. Courtesy of
     Hyperion Records Ltd., London. CDA67301/2.

9.   Benjamin Britten, *The Young Person's Guide to the Orchestra*
     © Boosey & Hawkes, Inc. From *Stokowski Conducts Music of the Twentieth Century*. (p)
     Music and Arts Programs of America, Inc.

10. Giuseppe Verdi, *Falstaff*
     From *Verdi—Falstaff*. Arturo Toscanini, NBC Symphony Orchestra. 1950. RCA Victor
     60251-2 RG. Courtesy of Sony BMG Music Entertainment.

11. Johann Sebastian Bach, *The Musical Offering*, "Ricercare a 6"
     From *Johann Sebastian Bach—A Musical Offering*. Performed by Music from Aston
     Magna, John Gibbons, fortepiano. . Courtesy of Centaur Records, Inc. CRC 2295.

12. Thomas Luis de Victoria (1548–1611), "O quam gloriosam est regnum in quo cum
     Christo gaudes omnes Sancti/Amici stolis albis sequunter Agnum quocunque ierit."
     ("O how glorious is the kingdom wherein all the saints rejoice!/Clothed in white
     robes they follow the Lamb whithersoever he goeth.")
     From *Victoria—Ave Maris Stella / O Quam Gloriosum*. Westminster Cathedral Choir.
     David Hill, conductor. Courtesy of Hyperion Records Ltd., London. GAW21114.

13. Ludwig van Beethoven, "Credo," *Missa Solemnis*
     From *Herbert von Karajan—Testament*. EMI Records SBT-2126. Courtesy of Testament.

14. Johann Sebastian Bach, "Credo," *Mass in B Minor*
     From *Bach B Minor Mass*. Robert Shaw Chorale and Orchestra. RCA Victor 0902635292.
     Courtesy of Sony BMG Music Entertainment.

15. Duke Ellington, "C Jam Blues"
    © Famous Music Corporation. From *Duke Ellington's Greatest Hits*. CK 065419. Courtesy of Sony BMG Music Entertainment.

16. Keb' Mo', "The Perpetual Blues Machine"
    © Keb' Mo' Music/Playin' Possum Music. From *Keb' Mo' Just like You*. Okeh/Epic ED67316. Courtesy of Sony BMG Music Entertainment.

17. Ludwig van Beethoven, Piano Concerto no. 5 in E-flat Major, op.73. (the "Emperor" Concerto)
    From *Solomon Testament: Beethoven: Piano Concerto No. 5 / Mozart: Piano Sonatas Nos. 11 & 17*. (2001). EMI Records SBT 1221. Courtesy of Testament.

18. Duke Ellington, "Satin Doll"
    © Tempo Music, Inc/WB Music Corp./Duke Ellington Music. From *Best of Duke Ellington*. Capitol Records. Courtesy of EMI Music.

19. Charlie Parker, "Moose the Mooche"
    © Atlantic Music Corporation. From *Jazz Masters: Miles Davis*. Laserlight 17 255. Licensed through Delta Entertainment Corporation, Los Angeles, California.

20. Ornette Colman, "Lonely Woman"
    © Phrase Text Music/MJQ Music, Inc. From *Duet: June Christy and Stan Kenton*. Capitol Jazz CDP 077 7 89285 2 2. Courtesy of EMI Music.

21. Arvo Pärt, "Silentium," *Tabula Rasa*
    © Universal Edition AG, Vienna/GEMA. From *Silencio*. Gidon Kremer. Nonesuch 79582. Courtesy of Warner Music Group.

22. Henryk Górecki, movement 1, Symphony no. 3 ("Symphony of Sorrowful Songs") for soprano and orchestra, op. 36
    © Boosey & Hawkes, Inc. From *Henry K. Górecki—Symphony No. 3*. Dawn Upshaw, soprano. London Sinfonietta, David Zinman, conductor. Courtesy of Warner Music Group.